Seeing
BEHIND
ENEMY
Lines

Seeing
BEHIND
ENEMY
Lines

**Exposing and Overcoming Satan's
Strategies Against Your Life**

APRILE OSBORNE

DESTINY IMAGE® PUBLISHERS, INC.

P.O. Box 310, Shippensburg, PA 17257-0310

"Promoting Inspired Lives."

This book and all other Destiny Image and Destiny Image Fiction books are available at Christian bookstores and distributors worldwide.

Cover design by Eileen Rockwell

Illustrations by Michael Santiago

For more information on foreign distributors, call 717-532-3040.

Reach us on the Internet: www.destinyimage.com.

ISBN 13 TP: 978-0-7684-4550-3

ISBN 13 eBook: 978-0-7684-4551-0

ISBN 13 HC: 978-0-7684-4553-4

ISBN 13 LP: 978-0-7684-4552-7

For Worldwide Distribution, Printed in the U.S.A.

1 2 3 4 5 6 7 8 / 23 22 21 20 19

Acknowledgements

ere I am writing acknowledgments when I am still in awe that this book is in your hands! First of all I want to thank Jesus, my Savior and my Lord for how He surprised me with all of this. He is such a good Father and He loves to surprise His kids with great gifts!

Second, I want to thank my parents Randall and Gaila Carroll. Thank you, Daddy, for always being my biggest fan. Even when I thought no one really cared or noticed you always showed the true Father's heart in how you loved me. To my amazing, praying, powerhouse momma who fought off every devil in my life when I didn't know how to do it myself and still today, thank you for always being there for me and the family. Mom, I am the woman I am today because of you! I honor and cherish you both more than you know and love you both so much! Daddy, just like I promised you, I will be busy about the Father's business until we meet again in Heaven.

I would like to thank my amazing husband, Chad Osborne. Babe, thank you for all the hours of agreeing with me in prayer and what seemed like thousands of hours editing these words. I could have never done this without your support and words of encouragement. You are a true gift to me and our family, standing on the Word of God for our lives. I love you!

To my incredible kids Kody, Kelton, and Kelsey, my son-in-law, Ryan, and my daughter-in-law, Anna, and all my beautiful grandbabies—Landon, Jaydon, Leilani, and Ezekel—thank you all for allowing me to make mistakes and for loving me without judgment! Thank you for supporting me. Thank you, Kody and Kelsey, for speaking life to me when I felt unqualified and beaten down. To my strong son, Kelton, thank you for being such an example of strength and love to me. You all taught me how to truly love, forgive, and encourage, and, more importantly, you helped me see how the Father can look in the faces of His children and find such joy in each of them! I love you guys to the moon and back!

I want to thank my spiritual grandfather and my "Papaw," Dr. Norvel Hayes, for taking me in as one of the family! Thank you for all the hours that you poured into me as I was growing up and all the times you told me to "just sit there and watch Holy Spirit move," which He always did so powerfully! Thank you for teaching me to resist the devil and to keep the Gospel simple. I love you, Papaw, and I'll keep on casting out devils in the name of Jesus until I see you again in Heaven.

Finally, a most sincere thank you to all the ones who have labored with me in the Spirit to get this book out—Apostle Ryan and Joy LeStrange, Robert and Eleanor Roehl, and Kevin and Kathi Zadai, and to Larry Sparks and Destiny Image for taking a risk on an unknown author! I honor and love you all!

Special thanks to artist Michael Santiago for the illustrations. Please contact him for any art and/or graphic needs at www.michaelsantiago.org or mikesanti@outlook.com.

Contents

Introduction 11

Chapter 1   The Enemy's Boardroom 21

Chapter 2   Death Blow 37

Chapter 3   In the Garden 57

Chapter 4   Port Invasion 71

Chapter 5   Jezebel's Eviction. 85

Chapter 6   Atmospheric Warfare 103

Chapter 7   Marked. 119

Chapter 8   His River 135

Chapter 9   A Thin Line. 149

Chapter 10   Molecules of Heaven 161

Chapter 11   Chain of Command 175

Chapter 12   Residue of Heaven 199

The

TRAVELER

A s you read this book, I pray that your eyes are opened and your spirit comes alive to what is going on around you and throughout the world. I am sharing these very intimate encounters not to give any attention to myself or to the enemy, but only to increase your understanding of how the spiritual world works. Most importantly I want you to know the real authority that you have when you partner with Jesus and His Kingdom.

We are partnering with one or the other, either God's Kingdom or Satan's. You must understand that the spiritual world is actually even more real than the natural world around us. The enemy would love for us to stay ignorant about how he works and he never wants us to learn the authority we have over him and his demons, but Paul said in 1 Corinthians 12:1, "Now concerning spiritual things, brothers, I don't want you to be ignorant" (WEB).

Some translations use the word *uninformed,* but both words there are very clear. Look at Hosea 4:6, which says:

> *My people are destroyed for lack of knowledge. Because you have rejected knowledge, I also will reject you from being My priest. Since you have forgotten the law of your God, I also will forget your children* (NASB).

You can see now why knowledge is so important; it is truly life or death. We must learn to identify when Satan attacks us and how to not only defend ourselves but go on the offensive to push back against him. The light within us will always overcome the darkness, and I believe the more we know about the devil's plans and strategies, the easier it will be for us to defeat him.

Years ago when my children were babies, as a new and very young parent I worried about the evil in the world and all the possible things that could happen to my kids and fear tried to come on me. Early one morning when my son, Kelton, was almost two years old and my daughter, Kelsey, was about two months of age, I was praying and the Lord spoke to me and said, "If you were in a war and you could know all the moves of the enemy before he made them, would that have any effect on your ability to win that war?" The answer, of course, is yes, you would never lose a war if you could send people ahead to stop every plot of the enemy before he even started it.

After I understood what He meant, I said, "How will I see the plots of the enemy over my children before they ever happen?"

His simple reply was, "Ask Me and I will give it to you." So I asked and, suddenly, it was like someone turned on a side of my brain that I had never accessed before. It was not like I heard the Lord speak every time; it was a knowing so real you could never convince me otherwise. I would see and know the plot ahead of time, cover my kids in prayer, bind the enemy, and then release the angels as the Word instructs. As soon as I would do that, that plot would be dismantled. Let me give you a specific example of this.

When Kelton was 12 years old, he was visiting some family in another state without me or my husband. One morning while he was away, I woke up very early in the morning and I knew someone around him was telling him some lies and was operating in a very wrong spirit. If he had started to believe those lies, it would have planted a seed in him that would have taken a miracle of the Lord to be delivered from, especially at such an impressionable age. I immediately jumped up and started praying and, as clear as day, I knew I was supposed to go get him. He was 12 hours away from me by car, so by 5:30 a.m. I was in the car heading north to get him. He was due to stay another week, but I was putting an end to that as soon as I could get there. The moment I arrived, I could see the struggle on him and I wrapped him in my arms and said, "Let's go home." Normally, he would have wanted to stay, but he was so grateful I was there. I stopped at a friend's house, took a shower, got back in the car and drove right back home those 12 hours with not the slightest feeling of tiredness. When God needs you to do something, He gives you the strength and grace to accomplish it, no matter how difficult. Looking back on that situation I know with complete certainty it was the Lord. On that ride home Kelton began to tell me everything I already knew that had started to happen, and by the time we were home we had prayed and refused to accept those lies, and that attack against his life had been prevented before it ever really got started.

This type of knowledge is so important. In fact, knowledge is one of the nine gifts of the Spirit listed in First Corinthians 12:8-10. Having knowledge can save you so much pain and suffering by keeping you out of the traps of the enemy. Again, you need to remember that the Lord is no respecter of persons and you too can have this same knowledge for your marriage, your children, your job or business, and in all walks of life. God doesn't want us to be open to surprise attacks; we can know all about them and how to defeat them before they come.

Many people have asked me how this started or when I was granted permission to travel from kingdom to kingdom. I can honestly say I don't have the answers to those questions. I must also say that many of the things I saw and heard are not explainable or describable with human words, but I will do my best to try and paint the pictures for you. I feel like how the man Paul described in Second Corinthians 12:2 must have felt because as Paul described the man's experiences, "whether in the body I do not know, or whether out of the body I do not know." I don't think I am special in any way and I believe anyone can have the same types of experiences I have had if they just ask. There is no secret formula or special prayer to pray, so I can only say one day when I stand in Heaven in front of our precious Lord I will ask Him those same questions. For now, I can tell you I am humbled and honored beyond words that He has allowed me to see behind the veil, and try to take you back to when it all started.

In 2015, my hunger level began to increase to understand more about the Kingdom of the Lord. I started asking God to teach me His ways and the ways of His Kingdom. I believe He laid that prayer on my heart after He instructed me to start reading the Psalms. Psalm 86:11 says:

Teach me Your way, O Lord; I will walk in Your truth; Unite my heart to fear Your name.

I wanted to know His truth. I desired as much knowledge and revelation as He would give me about how to be like Him and to walk with Him, without being oblivious to the world around me—the *real world* that is.

I grew up in a ministry that wasn't afraid to talk about that real world, the one that includes both the natural world that we can see, taste, and smell, but also the supernatural world that some people either don't know about or just refuse to believe actually exists. My spiritual father, Dr. Norvel Hayes, who was really more like an actual grandfather to me, taught me about the spiritual world, not from a standpoint of fear but of faith. He told me how crafty our enemy tries to be and the way he attacks and buffets us, but how we can walk in freedom and be victorious over him.

The Lord spoke to me and said, "Everything the enemy has to use against you I (Jesus) already defeated when I was on earth." He reminded me that the enemy cannot create anything, so he cannot come up with anything new. He can't invent any new ways to attack us, so he just tries the same things over and over in different ways. The Lord told me to research as much as I could about the enemy in the Word. At the same time, I also began to ask Holy Spirit to increase my spiritual IQ so that I would not believe the lies of the enemy nor fall for any of his dumb tactics.

Then, in 2016 I was in a private prayer meeting and a person there gave me a prophetic word that I would not understand until my "travels" began. In this word, the Lord spoke and said that I would start encountering His Kingdom and that I had been granted access to see and learn more about what is going on in the spirit realm. At the time, I felt it was a powerful word, but I couldn't even imagine the fullness of what it meant until now.

Ten days later I found myself in Phoenix, Arizona, at a conference where I was a part of a team that was there to serve another ministry. During those ten days, I had another man I had just met give me the same type of prophetic word. Overall it was a little different from the earlier word, but this time the Lord said I would "dangle between earth and Heaven" and be able to minister from this heavenly place. I knew that was a confirmation of what I had been asking for. As a side note, when anyone gives you a prophetic word of any kind it will usually be a confirmation of something you already know or have been seeking for. If it doesn't bear witness with the Holy Spirit in you, don't listen!

After that second word came, I began to seek even more understanding of His Kingdom and to learn of His ways of how to defeat the enemy. I am not sure if you've ever been around a young child learning and seeing everything for the first time. If you have, you know that they ask what seems like an endless stream of millions of questions. I have three amazing children and four grandchildren as of right now, so I have certainly experienced that inquisitive stage. At this point, I think the Lord looks at me like a two-year-old child who is always asking questions like "Why this?" or "What is that?"

I just don't want to get to Heaven and have the Lord look at me and say, "Why didn't you just ask? I wanted you to know so much more." The Bible, in Jeremiah 29:13, says, "And you will seek Me and find Me, when you search for Me with all your heart."

I love John 14:14, where Jesus says to His disciples, "If you ask anything in My name, I will do it." Some people may try to make things complicated, but I take the Bible at face value. I enjoy asking questions, and I enjoy it even more when He answers, so I encourage you to become an asker if you're not already. The enemy absolutely hates when we become a student of the Word and of Holy Spirit.

During this journey of truly seeking more knowledge and pressing into the things of the Spirit, I realized that the atmosphere around me in my prayer time was becoming what I would call "thicker," meaning I was aware that the spiritual world was more present. I knew that the enemy was getting upset with me, but also that there were more angels present than I had ever felt. Today, I realize when I began this quest to know more about these kingdoms, the enemy was not thrilled at all about my new hunger for knowledge and to learn how to easily defeat him, so he puffed himself up and came to intimidate me.

Why would he do that? The answer to your question is that the enemy has little spy spirits that report to him about your spiritual temperature and your hunger level. Look at it this way. If you work for someone else, your boss probably requires you to report in and give him or her status updates of your progress for whatever you're working on. It's the same way in the enemy's camp. He can't read our minds so he has to check in constantly to see if he needs to bother us or not. If he isn't bothering you, he isn't scared of you, and it's time to get your spiritual thermometer out to check yourself.

I believe as you read this book you will quickly see where your spiritual IQ is. Do not be intimidated or worried if you have no understanding of what I am talking about right now. Reading *Seeing Behind Enemy Lines* will show you how to ask and what you should be asking for. The Holy Spirit is your best teacher, so allow Him to walk you through His school and I promise you will never be the same.

CHAPTER 1

The ENEMY'S Boardroom

In the early hours of the morning on September 26, 2016, I was still asleep when a light in my bedroom caused me to open my eyes, and standing next to me was an angel. I had certainly been aware of angelic activity in a few instances before in my life, but I had never seen an angel in a full and tangible form before. The first thing I noticed were his crystal-like and strikingly green eyes that had an incredible shine and luster. They were sharp and piercing, yet I can best describe them as if love, peace, and acceptance radiated directly from them. I didn't notice much more about the angel at that moment because the presence of Heaven had filled the room.

The next thing I knew, the angel had taken my hand and we were instantaneously transported to a place above what appeared to be the boardroom of the enemy, almost as if we were looking in from a one-way window. The room I saw was about the size and shape of a large conference room, and in the middle of the room was a rectangular table with personalized places for each spirit to sit. Their seats were not marked with their names but each one was custom fitted for the size and shape of that spirit, and even their section of the table had an indentation cut out for them to slide into. On the table were what looked like papers or transparent documents and oddly enough a Bible. There was a gray hazy fog or smoke throughout the room, but not too thick to see through.

It seemed to be a staff meeting of some sort, and I could see and hear their discussion on what they think is happening now in the body of Christ. I noticed that there was one large spirit that was leading this meeting and the other spirits in the room were calling him "D." My angel looked over and said, "D is death and destruction." D was very tall and overall the largest spirit in the room. He had some type of clothing or material covering his legs, but his torso area was uncovered, except for a large emblem or badge strapped to his chest, and his general shape resembled a male human. His upper body was covered in sores that hung open all the way to his inner structure (I don't know if it is bone or another substance), similar to what I imagine an extreme case of leprosy would look like, but much worse. The sores were oozing some type of fluid and contained many tiny organisms that didn't seem to be harming D at all, but rather were worshiping him.

There were many lesser, or prince level, spirits in the room, all smaller than D, but different shapes and sizes from each other, and they did not seem to be any specific gender. They were enraged because of the increase of prayer from the local cities or areas they were assigned to and grumbling that orders and instructions between them were getting lost because of the sound that was rising from the earth and interrupting them.

Another elder leader, who was a little shorter than D and whose head was disproportionate to his body, told these prince spirits to follow the sound back to their cities and to launch attacks of despair, defeat, and hopelessness! He had two fingers missing from his left hand, as if they had been chopped off at some point in the past, and his skin was gray like the lungs of a long-time smoker. He told the other spirits, "The people praying don't know that they're causing such a disturbance against us." He began to laugh out loud in a very shrill yet confident tone and said, "Their ignorance always saves the day."

Many of the spirits in the room laughed as well, but another strongman spoke out and said, "Enough with this petty talk! How are we stopping what they are prophesying about the harvest?" and then he screamed, "I can see their faith has increased and we are losing many people to their crying out! It is causing us to step backward as they take our territories." This spirit was also gray and had a completely withered and paralyzed right arm. His whole body appeared to be deformed and his shoulder area was especially disjointed. He kept saying how their forces would be defeated if things continued this way and then he said, "He," talking about the Lord, "is teaching them that He is already in them to take us out."

Another spirit they called "Blind," a smaller spirit who had what looked like a very bad case of psoriasis, spoke up and said, "We just need to confuse them and keep them stupid." They all laughed and said, "That is easy!"

After that a very tall and attractive being walked in that appeared to be part male and part female. This spirit had very long legs and large feet and it was wearing boots with very sharply pointed tips. Its hair was long and thick and was wrapped around its body like a cape. They called this being "Jazz," and when it walked in, it took over the meeting and said, "I have been busy keeping them bound and in their own drama." Jazz explained how some believers see it but most still don't recognize it inside the Lord's house because it controls people through the shroud of religion.

My angel asked me, "Do you know Jazz?" and I said, "Yes, that is Jezebel." He smiled and said, "Yes," and then said, "Shhhh, listen," so my attention went back to the meeting. Jazz spoke of a group that is giving them problems and it called that group the "fasted ones." Jazz began to explain to them, "I cannot hide from them. I've tried coming and going from an area when a fasted one is around, but it doesn't work because they see my trail."

My angel said to me, "He (the Lord) already said 'And he who overcomes, and keeps My works until the end, to him I will give power over the nations…and I will give him the morning star.'" He handed me a star that went inside my chest and enlarged inside of me as I stood there.

As soon as the star was given to me, D stood up and said, "We have company."

My angel smiled and said, "Watch. Raise your right hand and speak now the word 'continue,'" so I did.

Right away the one named Blind said, "Come on, focus. Let's finish this. We need to get back to our stations." They all seemed distracted but regained their composure.

Jazz spoke up and said to D, "How do we defeat these fasted ones?"

D replied, "We do not take them on."

Jazz was angry at that answer and said, "I have spent too much time in those homes (to give up now)," but D said, "Stop it and move on." Jazz mumbled, "We will see."

Then D said, "Okay, so we are clear on what to do, let's keep it tight." He began to give out orders of pain, loss, and defeat. A large attack across the body of Christ was distraction and disunity, which he said to do by keeping them busy fighting amongst themselves. Then he turned and said to the main leaders, "Let's make them hungry for Babylon and keep the gossip juicy."

Then, all of a sudden, my spirit jumped and we were surrounded with an army of angels led by Michael. I'm not sure how I knew it was Michael specifically, but there was no doubt in my mind. He was very tall, maybe 14 feet or more, and he was slender but literally exuded strength and confidence. There was no fear or weakness in him at all. His very presence gave me a feeling of safety and peace even though I knew he was ready for war. The angel army stood silent and with what I would describe as a smirk on their faces. It seemed like about 25 seconds went by and then D and Jazz both stood and said, "We are not alone."

When he said that, Michael raised his right arm and motioned for a group of the angels to head into the meeting. The angelic division that Michael called was named "Wave." They surrounded the meeting and all of the spirits inside the meeting froze; they could not move. Then my angel said, "Let's go get a closer look," and the light inside me increased in intensity. I walked with him into the meeting and he said, "See, you can get up close for they have no strength or ability to move with us here."

I turned to ask, "How can we freeze them like this?"

He smiled and I could see inside my light that the face of Jesus was there and then my angel said, "You don't. He does." Then he said, "'Not by might nor by power, but by My spirit,' says the Lord of hosts." My angel continued, "This is a preview of 'The Lord will cause your enemies who rise against you to be defeated before you. They shall come out against you one way and flee before you seven ways.'"

Then from my light Jesus spoke and said, "The reason the Son of God appeared was to destroy the devil's work." As He spoke the enemies' faces became distorted. They could not look at us and sweat appeared on all of them. You could feel them tremble internally even though they couldn't move.

Then Michael raised his right arm again and the enemies split and left the room in all different directions.

As we walked back to my bedroom, just my angel and I, he said, "Remember your armor every day for it keeps you aware of and protected from the schemes of the enemy." He continued, "It's a gift of the Kingdom. You asked for the ways of the Kingdom so you will now begin to understand those ways."

Then he said, "Go on back now," but I said, "No, I want to stay and learn." I had a million questions running through my mind, but he said, "More later. Keep asking of Him and He will allow me to show you more of our ways."

I said, "Okay," and as I looked back from my bed I could see the faces of the angel army standing in the distance waiting for me to send them.

I still remember the emotions and the feeling in the room when I had that first encounter. I was in somewhat of a state of shock, of course, but at the same time I had total peace. I was never afraid, and I was immediately in anticipation of what I would be shown next as I began to reflect on what I had just seen and learned.

Something one of the strongmen said taught me so much. When he laughed and said, "Their ignorance always saves the day," I understood more than ever before why the Lord said through Paul, "I do not want you to be ignorant." Have you ever looked back and said, "Wow, I was so stupid when I did this or that"? Of course, we all have. Why do some have more knowledge than others? Why does it seem some people understand more than others? Are we all not made in the image of the Lord? We all have the same ability to know Him and be like Him. After hearing those demonic forces make fun of our lack of knowledge and awareness, I had an increase of hunger like never before come over me to make sure I was not one of those ignorant ones. I began to ask for knowledge, and you know He answers when we ask.

I also learned so much more about this spirit they called Jazz, and later in the book you will read about a huge victory for the Kingdom of God regarding Jazz. There are so many books and teachings out there about the spirit of Jezebel that I won't get into it much here, but I will say that spirit has been one of the most rampant in our churches for the past several years and that prayers of the believers against it are working.

Another thing that really affected me from this encounter was when they used the term "fasted ones." I knew immediately what they meant by that term, but it was so interesting to hear them referring to those who fast and pray as being able to see their "trail." It was clear that even the demonic kingdom understood the power of fasting and how it affects our spiritual IQ. I believe we must fast more than ever in these last days, and I should say that I am talking about fasting food. I'm not saying that it doesn't help to fast, or lay down, things besides food like TV, social media, or other things that our flesh likes, but every mention in the Bible about fasting is relative to food. Fasting in and of itself does not make us more spiritual or get us closer to God, but what it does is allow us to hear more clearly what God and Holy Spirit are saying to us. Fasting shows obedience and sacrifice through the crucifying of our flesh. Along with prayer and faith, fasting can do amazing things in our lives. Here are a few examples:

- We can fast for help in a particular situation or for a particular problem, as Esther did for herself and the rest of the Jews in Esther 4:15-16.

  Then Esther told them to reply to Mordecai: "Go, gather all the Jews who are present in Shushan, and fast for me; neither eat nor drink for three days, night or day. My maids and I will fast likewise. And so I will go to the king, which is against the law; and if I perish, I perish!"

- We can fast for direction and purpose or a specific need in our lives or in the life of someone else, like Daniel did throughout chapter 9 of his book. I would encourage you to read that entire chapter, but Daniel 9:3 says:

  Then I set my face toward the Lord God to make request by prayer and supplications, with fasting, sackcloth, and ashes.

- We can also fast for more power to overcome sickness or any other type of demonic attack as Jesus taught the disciples when they couldn't cast the devil out of the young boy in Matthew 17:14-21. In verse 21 He said, "However, this kind does not go out except by prayer and fasting."

What a powerful tool that we need in this hour, and I pray the enemy considers me as a "fasted one."

Next, let's discuss the star. My first question was why the star hitting my chest awakened the spirit that was leading the meeting, "D," to know we were in the room. This puzzled me for some time. I asked the Lord for clarity on this, and just recently He spoke to me about the power of His Spirit increasing in us and how that makes the enemy more aware of us and makes us more of a target. We all have been through things in life that caused pain or trauma that we need healing for or to be set free from. The Word is serious when it says things like: "'In your anger do not sin': Do not let the sun go down while you are still angry, and do not give the devil a foothold" (Eph. 4:26-27 NIV), or "casting all your cares [all your anxieties, all your worries, and all your concerns, once and for all] on Him, for He cares about you" (1 Pet. 5:7 AMP).

I could go on and on about this because it has become so real to me and you have to catch this to really increase in knowing Him and knowing of His Kingdom. When we carry around what I call "garbage," like past hurts or bitterness for example, it causes a blockage in us to be able to receive fully from the Lord. Think of it like this: when your kitchen sink won't drain because something is clogging up the pipe and blocking the flow of the water, everything gets backed up and we have to use some type of chemical or device to remove that clog for free-flowing water to drain through those pipes correctly. It's the same thing with us; all the things we hold on to and do not allow Him to heal or deliver us from, build up and block the river of living water from flowing out of our bellies. In this encounter, the star was like a super powerful Drano® for me. It cleaned me out or took the place of everything else, and as soon as that hit me there was no hiding the presence of the Lord inside of me. Everything on earth and in Heaven knows when His presence is on the scene. I have included some prayers at the end of this chapter that will bring the drain cleaner into your life so the flow of the Spirit can be restarted and the Light can shine through you.

I loved how the Lord revealed to me the authority I had over them with Jesus, the Light, inside me, even in their own boardroom. If He lives in you, you have all power over the enemy and his demonic powers. We can bind them and loose them, command them to leave us alone or stop attacking us, and deliver others from their power in the name of Jesus!

In this encounter, we can also see how the enemy releases attacks on us as the body of Christ. I am sure you can reflect back and think of times when you or someone you love have fallen victim to the types of attacks the demonic spirits were discussing. I know I have fought distractions in a big way, and you have to remember all distractions are not necessarily sinful. You can be busy or just caught up in day-to-day life and find yourself distracted from spending time with your Father. Even ministry itself can be what keeps us from getting alone with Him enough. After the enemy gets our primary focus off of God and our true purpose, it's easy for him to bring disunity in the body, and the next thing you know we as Christians start fighting amongst ourselves and we have little to no effect for the Kingdom of God or against the kingdom of darkness. We love the drama and the gossip so much that we miss the signs of these simple but effective attacks against us.

Another thing I learned for sure during this encounter is that when the army of the Lord shows up you know it and so does every evil spirit in that area. When Michael spoke to the division of the angels he called Wave, I felt a wind from Heaven that went through every part of who I am. I could feel the power they carried, which, of course, is sourced from Heaven itself. I'll talk more about Michael later in the book.

As I entered the meeting room I had a new understanding of what the Word means when it talks about abiding in Him and Him abiding in me and what that actually looks like. It was so powerful to see how the enemy is paralyzed by His presence, and it reminded me once again that without Him we are nothing. The power of the Lord's voice had such an effect on them that it actually distorted their appearances and you could feel the fear they have toward Him. Even though they couldn't move, you knew they were trembling on the inside. No evil spirit has any power against Him and they know it!

The last thing I took away from this first encounter came from the angel that had traveled with me. I have been careful each day since then to remember to put on the armor of God because it gives you a sense of being covered and strengthened at all times. Seeing a glimpse of the spirit world and the warfare that is going on in unseen realms will have you wanting to protect yourself as much as possible. I feel almost like I'm putting on a set of x-ray glasses to let me see the attacks of the enemy before they come and my faith is increased to block them by the power of the Holy Spirit.

Needless to say, when the angel told me if I asked to see more he would be allowed to come get me again, I didn't waste any time asking, and my second encounter came just a couple of weeks later.

PRAYER FOR THE ARMOR
(FROM EPHESIANS 6:11-18):

Lord, I put on the whole armor of God as Your Word instructs me, that I may be able to stand against the wiles of the devil. Lord, I will not wrestle against flesh and blood, but in Your name I will have victory over principalities, over powers, over the rulers of darkness of this world, and over spiritual wickedness in high places. I place the helmet of salvation on my head and I declare I have the mind of Christ, that I can retain and recall all that I have studied and know to be true according to Your Word only. I put on the breastplate of righteousness to keep my heart covered so that I may not sin against You and I wrap the belt of truth around me so that I can always be aware of what is and is not of You. I pick up the sword of the Spirit, which is Your Word, so I may be able to speak Your truth from my mouth at all times and flow from deep within me. Lord, I take up the shield of faith and wrap it around me on all sides so that I can extinguish every blazing arrow thrown at me by the enemy. I step into the Gospel of Your perfect peace that passes all understanding and place it on my feet so that I may be a carrier of that peace. In Your armor, I will be able to subdue the enemy and overcome all of his evil plots. Thank You, Jesus, for this armor and I pray all of this passionately in Your name, amen.

PRAYER TO BREAK ANY DEMONIC PARTNERSHIP THAT YOU MAY HAVE MADE, KNOWINGLY OR UNKNOWINGLY:

Lord, I cry aloud and ask You to allow Your Spirit of truth to come and bring a light into anything dark that is hidden in me or my family! Only Your pure love reveals all things and heals all things. Jesus, forgive me if I have partnered with the enemy and have allowed him to work through my life in any way. I ask that Your blood that washes away all sin come and wash me, cleanse me, and remove any impure thing that might have rooted itself in me. I plead that blood over myself, over my children (name your children and other family members you are praying over), over my home, and over all that You have given me or placed under my authority and stewardship. I will only partner with You, Jesus, in all things and for who You have created me to be. I partner with You in my marriage, in my home, in my job or business, and every area of my life. Holy Spirit, come like a river and teach me all things about the Kingdom of God so that I may walk in heavenly places with You and my Father.

*Satan, I break every demonic contract or agreement I have made with you! I denounce any lie that I may have believed to be true that you have told me. You are **not** allowed in my* *life, my thoughts, my mind, my family, my home, or anything that belongs to me. You have* **no** *more authority over me. I will not partner with you and your evil spirits anymore. I see now and understand that I am a child of the most High God, and you cannot torment me and my family ever again. Go from me and never return!*

Now, just take a few moments to worship and thank the Lord for how good He is! Make a new commitment to your prayer life and keep your armor on at all times. You are His beloved!

CHAPTER 2

Death
BLOW

was awakened to the sweet presence of Holy Spirit and I looked immediately at the clock beside my bed—it was 5:57 a.m. on October 18, 2016. Holy Spirit said to me, "It's five fifty-seven," and then repeated that twice more.

I wasn't sure why He was emphasizing the time, but I knew He had something for me so I began worshiping as I lay there for about 30 seconds. I said to Him, "Do You want me to get up to pray?"

He said, "No," and then my angel came and said, "Let's go."

I said, "Okay, where?" and he said, "You asked for more."

Instantly we were back over the same meeting room as in my first encounter. I saw no one in the room, only the gray haze that I had seen before. Then, all of a sudden, I saw a small but very demonic spirit come into the "boardroom." He could not stand up straight and he had a single spike coming out of his back. He was dragging a person into the room by her hair, but the person was not someone I knew. It was a young female who seemed to be around 15 to 18 years of age. I knew the girl was ashamed, broken, and hurting and had given up. As soon as he dropped the girl down, a face appeared out of the left side of the room that was very evil. It was not a demon I had ever seen, but he had such anger in his eyes toward this girl and I knew he hated her. He began to yell, saying, "I have found you guilty!" Then he called her liar, cheater, fornicator, and thief, told her she was not worthy of love. He carried on, saying "I find you worthless and unqualified." As these words came out of the face's mouth they had weight with them and as they hit her you could see wounds appear on her.

Suddenly, a different face appeared out of the right side of the room with a bright light that pushed back the gray haze that was in the room. The demon with the spike in its back immediately ran out of the room, but the other dark face remained. The bright face spoke and silenced the dark face. He began to woo the girl, and he called her beloved. As soon as he called her beloved the evil face spoke again to her, "You're nothing but a liar," but the angel said to the girl, "He is the liar and the father of all lies."

Then the evil spirit said, "You're a cheater," but the heavenly face responded to her, "I have the blood of Jesus that covers all for you. He sees you as beautiful, as a gift, and as a jewel."

As soon as he said the word *jewel*, I could sense that she was longing inside to turn to the angel but she was only able to barely attempt to sit up. The bright face had kept his focus on the girl and gave no attention to the enemy, but at this point he raised his gaze and gave a look of force with no words and the enemy's face disappeared suddenly. I could see that the young girl was wanting to get up but was so weakened and in such great pain she couldn't do it alone. Then, from the right side of the room, a group of five angels surrounded her. As they did she became lost within their wings and you could see they were strengthening her to stand on her own. They all arose together, and as they stood I could see that the angels and the girl almost appeared to be one person. As soon as she stood the evil face returned on the left to say something, but she turned and gave the demonic face the exact same look of force that the heavenly face had given earlier, again with no words, and again the face disappeared. Then the room was empty.

I looked at my angel and he said to me, "This is the war over them. Stay tender and compassionate toward them."

I asked, "What made the angels come to help her?" and he answered, "When you or others like you show up, you bring the angels to war."

Then there appeared another group of angels who walked into the room from the right side and they just passed through the room from right to left. Again, I looked at my angel for an explanation and he said, "Watch," and

then here came the army of the enemy. They were being led by the one they call D. They walked in order like they were marching to a beat of some type, but I could not hear the sound. Some were small, some were older in appearance, some were tall and large, some were attractive in nature, but most were indescribable because they were so ugly. They came in and said, "We are here!" and all began to laugh. "'They try to intimidate us!"

D said with a loud voice. "Are you intimidated?"

All those present raised their weapons and their arms and shouted, "No, we are not!" and the laughter broke out again.

They all sat down to have a meeting and the little spirit that dragged the girl in earlier was griping to D that he lost her to the angel. He began to state his case—that he had brought her in defeated and ready for the last blow—but how suddenly this angel had appeared, messing it all up for him. Then Jazz came in, mad at that spirit and complaining to D about him. As Jazz spoke about him, the spike on his back began to disappear and then he began to bend over and shrink like he was dying right there before them all. Finally, he just disappeared because he withered away into nothing. I looked at my angel and asked, "What just happened?"

He said, "Their words can only cause death, even to each other or about each other."

D then called for a new spirit to replace the one that vanished, so another one came and took a seat and D called for the trainer to come to give him some pointers. When that demon walked in, its bottom half looked human and its top half was devil-like. I looked at my angel and asked, "Is that human?" and he said, "Yes, he is possessed."

This new spirit, the trainer, sat down and began to give pointers on how to possess people. He first corrected them by telling them to not only go for the mind. The "trainee" demon asked, "Where do I get one that will let me possess it?"

With a smile, the trainer answered, "The church house."

The trainee said, "What? Really? Not a worldly one?"

The trainer said, "No, let them alone," and he continued to give instructions as follows: "Find a stronger one and use them to hurt the weaker ones and then go after the weak one once they have been wounded by the 'beloved one' (or stronger one)."

Jazz spoke up and said, "I will come into the atmosphere of that church to weaken them for the attack."

An older demon that was not present before came in from the left side. He was short and stocky, with a definitive muscular structure and he appeared to be strong and intimidating. He had some sort of deformity on the side of his face where you would normally expect to see an ear, and I had the immediate impression that he was highly intelligent. You could tell he was a "boss," a leader, so much so that in my mind I questioned if it was Lucifer himself, not just from the way he looked, but because of how the atmosphere of evil in the room grew more intense upon his arrival. Even though I didn't say that out loud, my angel looked at me and said, "No, that is not Lucifer."

I replied, "Who is he?" but my angel said, "That is not for you to know yet."

D, who was sitting at the head of the table got up and this new demon took his chair. He looked at Jazz and said, "You don't even know you have been exposed. You have been in the White House since 1995 and have had free reign throughout America but now you have been identified and you are losing." (After I woke up I researched that year and I learned that was when Monica Lewinsky was hired as an intern and her affair with Bill Clinton began.)

His words came out with so much anger that D went over to the boss and, although he whispered in his ear, I could hear him say, "Don't say that. You will destroy her."

Jazz had already begun to take on the appearance of death and you could see it had lost some strength. Boss said to D, "Jazz will be defeated again." Then with confidence he said, "But you have not yet worked with Delilah! Even His prophets don't see her coming." D was satisfied with that.

Boss gave some brief instructions to the group such as how to keep "them," the Christians, wounded and caught up in drama until Delilah is fully released. At that moment the thought crossed my mind, "Lord, don't let us be deceived," and, as if he heard my thought, the boss stood up quickly and said, "They are listening."

They all got up, got back into their line, and marched out with the same formation that they came in with. Not one word was spoken out because they knew we were listening. I looked at my angel and he said, "You see, this all has to do with the kingdoms. The Lord sent the enemy to earth and this has been his kingdom, but the fight has begun to establish His Kingdom on earth as it is in Heaven." He explained that this must happen so that His Spirit can come onto all flesh as was prophesied by Joel. Continuing, he said, "This is a battle that has not yet been fought because it's for the last days, when the sons and the daughters will prophesy, the old men will have dreams and the young men will see visions."

I asked, "Are we in tribulation?" and he said, "We have been in tribulation."

Suddenly we were in front of a large screen and scenes of Christians being martyred, scenes of people dying in war, and scenes of other violence were flashing across the screen quickly. I was crying because of what I saw, but then the screen split and behind the screen were the gates of Heaven. We were just outside the gates. My angel looked at me and said again, "We have to establish His Kingdom on earth as it is in Heaven. Let's go see the Kingdom."

I would relate the tour that came next to a backstage pass. The gates opened and I put my foot on the golden street. As soon as I did, I felt immediately as if I was one with the place. I realized Heaven is in you; it is a part of you and you are a part of it. In the atmosphere you could see gold particles floating in the air and my angel told me to breathe it in. He told me that the reason the enemy had fought me with my breath (I've had asthma issues before in my life and again recently) is because he didn't want me to experience breathing in things like this. He told me to breathe it in several more times, and as I did I could feel something was happening in my lungs.

As we walked further in, there was a group of angels to the right playing with large gemstones as if they were snowballs. They were laughing and throwing the gems back and forth. My angel looked at me and said, "You can have joy like you own it," and in his hand there appeared a large red gem, which I assumed to be a ruby. He then said, "Joy is something that you own, something that you have, like this gem. You wear it like clothing and no one can take it from you."

As we moved forward, there was a group of children that looked to be between the ages of five to ten coming toward us. I could hear them talking and laughing. One of the younger boys came up to me and introduced himself as John. I told him my name was Aprile and he said, "I know you, Aprile! You must simply believe like I do." He repeated the words *just believe* several times, really singing it.

Then the oldest boy came up to me and introduced himself as John also. He said, "Believe in this Kingdom so you can have it on earth, on earth as it is in Heaven. I know on earth it is hard to see this Kingdom because you are under the influence of that kingdom. Close your eyes and see the Kingdom in you to establish it through you on earth. It's all about what you believe."

I had an immediate feeling like I was the boss, almost an owner, of Heaven and I had the thought, "Am I even allowed to feel this way?" I felt empowered.

After that I realized there was a sound there like music. I couldn't see a band, but I could see the actual sound waves in the air and all of Heaven—the grass, the trees, and everything around me—was moving to the rhythm of the sound. My angel turned to me and said, "It's the sound that builds, that heals, and that releases the Kingdom."

Suddenly I was back in my bed and he was standing next to me. He said, "Who is John to you?" and I said, "John is the one that prepared the way for Jesus to come."

He said, "That's right, and you now have been given a gift like John's and that is why the Lord has given you the word 'open up ye gates, for the King of Glory is coming in.'" I woke up at that time, and throughout the day what I had seen stayed heavy on my heart so I continued to pray and meditate.

Seeing the young girl in the boardroom and how the enemy plots against us increased my understanding about the different levels of demonic attacks. It is very disturbing how they team up against us. The more you see the plans of the enemy and learn the games he and his demons play, the easier it is to avoid falling into his traps. Their goal is to bring us into a place of such defeat that they can administer what they call the death blow.

Later in this book I will go into that more, but in short, when we think of the word death the first thing we associate with that is no longer being alive. They would love for that to happen, but they do not have that much power or control over us directly, so they want to deal a death blow to our mind, will, and emotions and to any areas of our lives we will allow them to have access to. For example, if the enemy can bring hurt, disunity, rejection, pride, and abandonment into your family by causing you or your spouse, parents, or children to partner with the wrong spirits and push away those who care for you the most, he can bring death to the family unit. From those broken relationships, he can bully someone into believing even more of his lies, taking them further away from God and His will for their lives until he gets them to a place of total defeat. That is where the spirits of depression and suicide can take over and the death blow can be finally dealt.

The enemy is after your identity. He has to make you believe you are not worth anything, that your gifts and talents have no value, and that you have no chance to make a positive impact for the Kingdom of God. He wants to make you think God doesn't want you or need you so you won't even try to fulfill the plan of God for your life, and if you come into agreement with that lie your identity can die. The devil is so strategic with his attacks, but the good news is he has no place or authority in our lives if you don't allow him to.

I asked Holy Spirit why the angels and the girl I saw appeared to be united as one. He talked to me about unity and reminded me of the prayer that Jesus prayed right before He went to the cross:

> *That they all may be one, as You, Father, are in Me, and I in You; that they also may be one in Us, that the world may believe that You sent Me. And the glory which You gave Me I have given them, that they may be one just as We are one: I in them, and You in Me; that they may be made perfect in one, and that the world may know*

that You have sent Me, and have loved them as You have loved Me (John 17:21-23).

Of course, we are not one with angels, but I believe this was just a visual example for me to see how, when we submit to Him, we become one with Jesus.

In my hunger to understand more, Holy Spirit continued to speak to me about us being *in* Him. The Word says several times that we can abide in Him and Him in us. If He is in us and we are in Him, that is the deepest kind of unity, and that is the relationship He desires. He tells us that by abiding in Him we can "bear much fruit" (John 15:5), or in other words be successful in all areas of our life as a testimony to Him being in control of our lives. In that same verse He also says that without Him we can't do anything, proving the absolute necessity of this closeness and relationship with Him.

In the passage from John 17, Jesus was praying for all believers then and in the future to be able to be one with Him like He is one with the Father. That means He wants us to be totally joined with Him and inseparable from Him, so that every person we encounter also encounters Him. His ultimate goal is for as many to see Him as possible so they can also become one with Him.

Maybe you are thinking, "How can Jesus abide in me? How can I live in Him? What does it mean for me to lose my life so I can find it? What do I do to die so that I can truly live?" The Bible says that there are mysteries that we will not understand, and we begin to rely on what our natural mind can process. We get caught up with what we can analyze or figure out on our own and lose focus on what the Word of God says or the sweet whispers of Holy Spirit are teaching us. When we make that choice to go with what makes the most sense to us, we stop asking, we stop longing for more, and we settle with accepting less than He wants us to experience. Why do we allow our brains to lead us in so many different directions, leaning on only logic or what we see or feel? God doesn't work with our natural minds or thoughts, nor does He function through our feelings or emotions. To be one with Him, we have to turn all that off. We have to lower ourselves, put aside any fears or anxiety, and simply trust in Him! When you actually know Him, and I mean really know Him, there is no way you can *not* trust Him. Make sure you are pursuing a real relationship and not just a handout.

God's plan for our lives is actually much more simple than we make it out to be. The enemy would love to keep us all in the place of confusion, chasing our own tails so to speak, but we can learn to block him out and ignore the lies he speaks over us or puts in our heads. We can pray for our thoughts to be the same as God's thoughts, and our ways to be the same as His ways, and we can become completely one with Him.

In this encounter you see that the enemy plots for our lives and how he can take us out. I look back on my own life and I can tell you stories of how some of his plans were executed over a period of ten years. It isn't always an obvious attack. He is patient to wait, to scheme, and to win only small victories over time until he thinks you're ready to be dragged in for that final death blow.

Most of us can remember a time when we were at a break-ing point, when we thought about giving up on everything that had any meaning to us. Perhaps you have even made an attempt to take your own life. We all have stories we could share that would shock each other. It is in the moment when those attacks come that we must have the knowledge and the prayer life to stand, to continue to abide in Him even through the storm. The Bible says in Proverbs 4:21, "Do not let them [His words] depart from your eyes; keep them in the midst of your heart." Keep the Word of God in front of you and stand firm on its promises because it works every single time.

If Jesus Himself used the Word and the Word only to defeat the enemy, why do we try other tactics? Do you think you know more than He does? Did the devil come up with a new attack on you that Jesus never defeated? No, of course not! Satan cannot create anything new so every attack he tries to bring has already been beaten unless we allow it to win. Stop trying to fight the enemy in your own strength or with your own "smarts" because you will fail continuously. You must have the Word of God inside of you so it can be constantly in your heart, in your mouth, in your emotions, and in every single fiber of who you are.

Just as we see how the enemy lies to us and the effects of those negative words, we also see from this encounter the power of the truth and the love of the Father for every one of us. He is always wooing us so sweetly and gently, drawing us closer to become one with Him. He is truly the lover of our souls, of everything we are. He is the only one who knows how to reach those places we may have even hidden from ourselves. He is the true Rescuer and the true Deliverer, our Healer, the Master of us all. Submitting to Him allows Him to defeat the enemy for us, to rebuke the devourer in our lives, and then wrap us up in His arms of love and protection.

The angel's answer when I asked why the other angels came to help the girl in the boardroom changed my thought process and behavior toward others. We need to understand that we as the Redeemed of the Lord carry Heaven with us. We carry light into darkness. If we walk in the authority we have through His Kingdom to affect the earthly kingdoms, we can be much more effective to those around us. We can even bring in the angels of war to any situation for ourselves or for others. Like Jesus, we must pursue the outcasts, the hurting, and the downtrodden. We can't just walk by and do nothing, allowing Satan to deal a death blow when we have the Answer they need. If the enemy can keep us down we will not be effective for the Kingdom. We have to stay free ourselves to be able to help others get free. We have to be strong to pull others up out of their pit.

It was so interesting to see the level of confidence the demonic forces have in their plots and schemes. As I looked back in my own life, I saw how quickly some dumb drama caused me to get distracted from my calling or my purpose. They even laughed at the idea of us thinking we are intimidating them or causing them to change course from their plans. In our own power, we have no effect on them, but when we allow God to invade us and His Kingdom to invade the earth, they are swiftly defeated.

Another thing that really impacted me was the visual display of Proverbs 18:21 where it says, "Death and life are in the power of the tongue." I could see death happening right in front of me from their words alone. Just picture every negative word coming out of your mouth doing physical harm to the person you are talking to or talking about. That is why gossip is so dangerous. You don't think about how speaking against someone is actually partnering with hell in the spiritual realm to cause hurt and death to that person. The enemy never speaks anything positive over anyone, so while his words are constantly trying to tear us down, we must be more mindful to keep our words positive and life giving. One of the enemy's easiest and most effective ways of entrance into our lives to cause us pain is by us partnering with him to cause pain to others.

I also want to talk about the defeat of Jezebel in the government of the United States of America. I understand "she" is not completely gone yet and there is a residue of her in some areas of government, but I believe that spirit has been exposed and is losing much of the control and influence she has had over all seven mountains of influence. Also, I am not saying this spirit is a purely sexual spirit, but she certainly uses every means she can to gain the control and position she seeks.

Let me be clear that this is not a political statement. When the news broke about President Clinton and Monica Lewinsky it released national and even worldwide open conversation about what is really sex and sexual sin. There were constant debates about the morality of relationships outside of marriage. I was a teenager at that time and I remember how this conversation reached even into the schools. In the media, the focus was whether or not what was admitted by

Mr. Clinton was actually sex, instead of the sin of adultery itself. At the time it seemed that not even the church leaders were responding or standing up for what was right. Ministers didn't even want to say the word sex because it was viewed as evil, so while the world was discussing it openly, the Christians said nothing. Now I'm sure Christians and church leaders were talking about it privately, but the enemy made a very public and high-level move and, as a whole, the body of Christ did not come together to do anything about it. There should have been an uprising against such an overtly sinful act in the highest office in our nation, even like the protests in the past against racial inequality and others, but instead it went unpunished.

I believe that is why Jezebel was given the national and even global authority it has operated in for the past several years. Shortly after that event you began to see many major church leaders being exposed for fornication, adultery, and even homosexuality. Church splits became more common as division grew in the body of Christ. I believe the fear of God and reverence left many churches and respect for both religious and government leaders was significantly diminished. The controlling spirit caused a total lack of unity within the body of Christ, which has led to more "church hurt" and people running away from God and the church than ever before.

However, I believe that over the most recent couple of years many men and women of God have received new revelation about Jezebel and have begun to educate us all about that spirit, which is why the "Boss" demon told it that it was identified and losing its influence. There are some great books and sermons out there that teach about how to recognize and overcome this spirit. I believe that the timing of this is important and we as the body today have a high level of authority to remove Jezebel and its residue completely out of our lives.

I thought it was very interesting what was said about the Delilah spirit and I asked Holy Spirit about it. He revealed to me that she was more confident than Jezebel because she was victorious in her plot against Samson, but Jezebel was defeated by Elijah and ultimately by Jehu. The devil cannot create anything new, so the same spirits we fight now are the same spirits we find in the Bible. The Word tells us that Delilah successfully tricked Samson and received her reward from the enemy, but she was not destroyed like Jezebel was. That is why the demonic spirit told Jazz it would be "defeated again."

There were a lot of different things that happened during this encounter, and certainly the best part was my brief look into Heaven itself. When you experience Heaven, you cannot accurately describe its wonder. I am still in total awe even thinking about and trying to write about what I saw. Everything there is, of course, beautiful, but the word that most resounds in me about Heaven is purity. I felt the very essence of God all around me and *perfection* is not a strong enough word. I will talk more about Heaven in later chapters but even your wildest imagination won't be a fraction of how wonderful it is in reality.

Lastly, meeting the different Johns gave me insight that I never had before. Think of it like this—the world needed John the Baptist to prepare for the arrival of Jesus. There is always a John or many Johns involved in the moving of the Kingdom to prepare the harvest. They are stirring up the atmosphere and making the Gospel known to all who have ears to hear. We must be like John and do everything we can to help establish God's Kingdom on earth as it is in Heaven.

CHAPTER 3

In the
GARDEN

I t was sometime in the afternoon on October 25, 2016, and I began to pray and worship. I could feel the Holy Spirit sweep over me and, in that moment, I closed my eyes. As I did, I was in a garden full of many different types of trees, flowers, and foliage, and much more beautiful than any garden I could ever imagine. The colors there were magnified, multi-dimensional, and more vibrant than anything I had ever seen. Simply looking at the colors was like being drawn deeply into them. The colors were like strength to me and carried healing and wisdom in them. I knew I was walking with my angel, so I said, "Where are we?" He turned and looked at me with the biggest smile and I smiled back and said, "What?"

With a laugh in his voice he said, "You have been given the garden."

Then I saw another angel, a warrior angel, tall and broad chested with a chiseled face and wearing full armor, standing in a place that appeared to be an exit or entrance. I looked up at him and he turned and said, "You have been invited here." With a smile, he looked at my angel and waved him on to go further into this place they called the garden.

As we walked I could feel the grass between my toes and it felt like I was walking on a soft, fleecy blanket. Many types of flowers were there, all in full bloom, and I realized there was a sound being created from within them. I stopped and gathered a few together, not pulling them out or picking them, just holding them to listen to their sound. The sound was like the soft whisper of a wind instrument, when your breath vibrates across the reed. The longer we stayed listening to this healing sound, I realized I didn't just hear it, but I could actually feel the breeze of the sound inside me, like it was purifying everything within me. My angel said, again with a smile, "Come on, we have a lot to see."

We strolled through a large group of trees and I saw that they were all connected by one enormous root, like they all grew there together at one time from one seed. I wondered how that was possible with so many trees; it seemed that there were hundreds or even thousands of them. I got down and crawled around under the trees, exploring their roots, and I followed them to a beautiful stream of water with a bluish iridescence. There were many streams in the garden, and they all led to a larger river.

As I stood at the bank looking back toward the trees and the roots, my angel said, "He created all things to gather together in this season." As he said "season," I could see all the roots of everything in this garden and it appeared like they were all tied together, feeding each other and drawing from the streams.

I said to him, "How does this happen? How does one not overpower and take more nutrients from the weaker ones?"

He said with a huge smile, "There is no limit. If one is hungrier than another, there is more than enough for all who trust."

Then he took my hand, and when he did I could hear the Father say, "I am gathering all things in Heaven and earth unto Me." As He said that, Ephesians 1:10 came to my mind. I knew my angel saw the scripture appear to me because he gets excited when I get a revelation of what the Lord is saying.

When I turned to my angel he said, "Study this out more. You will see it's Him gathering all things here (in Heaven) and there (on the earth). You will see all things are to flow to His rhythm."

He pointed to the stream and I could see it moving to an actual beat with a specific tempo, and the sounds from all over the garden began to converge into one new sound as they poured out into the river. The river flowed away from where we were standing and I could not see the end. I said to my angel, "Let's go see where the river leads."

He began to laugh out loud and said, "He told me you always want to jump ahead."

I couldn't help but laugh also, and I said, "I am working on that."

Then I heard my Father say, "I love that which I have placed inside of you." As He spoke to me I could feel His warmth and a closeness to Him like I had never felt before. It was like I was the only one on His mind and all of Him was talking to all of me.

I began to cry with joy and so did my angel. He said, "I love seeing the Lord enjoy you."

When he said that to me, I asked, "Enjoy me?"

He motioned with his hand around the garden and said, "This is the place He built for you and others to walk with Him in the cool of the day, because He enjoys being with you so much."

I immediately turned and asked, "Is this the Garden of Eden?"

A smile was on his face that I could get lost in, and he said, "You are in the garden of Heaven built in Eden." (In other words, as I understood it, Eden was the name of the city or the place where the "Garden of Eden" of Adam and Eve was located. The garden was actually Heaven on earth so after the fall of Adam the garden no longer existed on earth, which is why it has never been found.)

I looked puzzled again but I was not able to contain the joy I felt and I started laughing because the place was such a happy place. We were both laughing and we put our feet in the river. When we did I could feel the flow of the river almost like I was laying under it or immersed in the water. I instantly knew the river's speed, its temperature, its beat; I could feel the garden pulling on this river for its life and the nutrients flowing through it. It is very hard to describe, but the closest word I can use is *pure*. The life-giving power of the river to everything in the garden was such a pure, clean feeling.

Suddenly, out of a thick section of the trees came a group of angels I had never seen before. They appeared strong but were not warrior angels, and they came to where we were with a look of joy on their faces. One of them said to me, "Aprile, this is His river coming to the earth. Just as He showed John, He also shows His bride."

My angel said, "Revelation 22."

I said, "Ok I will study that too."

He said, "This is the cool of the day, where He has called you to Himself. You are here to be taught and take what you learn with you." Before I could reply he said, "Let's go, Chad (my husband) is coming home to you." He smiled and said, "You will bring others to this garden, and one day it will be established on earth again as it is here in Heaven." As soon as he said that I was back in my home and one minute later my husband walked in the door.

When my angel said, "You have been given the garden," something happened to me that I did not realize in the moment. It was not until later that I received a revelation of the meaning of that statement. You see, it's not about the physical place; it's about the intimate relationship with your Father. It's about the ability to walk with God with unfettered access. As soon as you understand the power and fulfillment from walking with God in this place called the garden, your spirit and soul will long for that type of relationship.

From the beginning, the enemy was jealous of the garden itself, but most importantly he was jealous of what it stood for—the relationship God had with Adam and Eve. God walking with man in the cool of the day infuriated him. That used to be his place; the daily walk with God was his before he fell. The enemy will never again be able to feel that peace, joy, and love. He can never again experience the fullness of the garden and God's presence. I know he now realizes what he lost and he wants nothing more than to try to keep us from experiencing that Presence that he no longer can. Satan's jealousy of us and of the love that God the Father has for us is what empowers him to continue to wage war against us.

There are three things about the garden that I was aware of immediately:

1. Everything there was life giving and the garden imparts life itself into the atmosphere.

2. Each thing contained in the garden had a unique sound and was releasing that sound into the air where all of the sounds of all the things gathered together to become sound waves or frequencies.

3. The sounds and the indescribable aromas of the place were penetrating every fiber of my being in a way that I had never experienced.

My husband and all three of my adult children are involved in worship in some way, either playing an instrument or singing, so there is always a sound of Heaven around me and worship has always been a big part of my life. There have been times when I was standing right next to a loud speaker and the sound coming out felt like it was vibrating my inner being. Now imagine something like that, but instead of the feeling coming at you from the outside of your body, in the garden it feels like your spirit is part of the sound and comes alive as the sound and vibrations permeate you from the inside out. The frequency of the Spirit inside you matches exactly with the frequency of Heaven.

God is calling us to walk with Him in true intimacy. Believe it or not, He wants us to know Him on the same level that He knows His own Son. Jesus says in John 7:29, "But I know Him, for I am from Him, and He sent Me." We are also "from Him" to be ministers of His Gospel to the world. It is such a special and private relationship; you are truly hiding in Him, being one with Him. No one can lay hands on you or pray for you to have this type of connection with the Father; it is solely in your control. We are not of this world; we are of His Kingdom and when you encounter it and encounter Him, you immediately know you were created in that environment. It is only then that you truly understand the definition of home. You never want to leave His presence. Your desire becomes to learn how to bring that Kingdom here to earth and walk with Him like that everywhere you go.

Understanding that we can walk and function in that Kingdom here on earth right now is a life-changing thought process. We can enter into the secret place with God, to capture His glory and become a carrier of it in the world. Just as I felt that the atmosphere of the garden was purifying every cell of my being, that is what we must have on earth. We live in the world surrounded by evil and this is the enemy's kingdom. The Bible says in Ephesians 2:2 that he is prince of the power of the air and First John 5:19 says that the whole world is under the control of the devil, so even though we are children of God and will be eternal residents of His Kingdom, we still reside here on earth in Satan's kingdom. However, if we obey the Lord in Second Corinthians 6:17 to "Come out from among them and be separate," that is the first step to seeing the reality of Luke 11:2 when Jesus told us to pray "Your Kingdom come. Your will be done on earth as it is in Heaven." It is clear from His Word that we can truly be in this world but not of it, meaning although our physical bodies are on the earth, we can live and operate in the realities and power of Heaven.

Can you see why the enemy and this world hate us so much? In John 15:19, Jesus says, "If you were of the world, the world would love its own. Yet because you are not of the world, but I chose you out of the world, therefore the world hates you." He chose us! That means to accept a different way of living all we have to do is choose Him back. We have been given access to go into a personal, secret place and get alone with God, to have encounters with Him and with Heaven itself, and to carry and release His manifested glory here on earth. That should give you a wake-up call to the level of authority we really have because the Kingdom we can call on is so much more powerful and real than the kingdom we walk around in. So many believers never find their garden or their encounter with Jesus here on earth. They don't fully understand that, since the veil of the temple was torn at the death of Jesus, there is no longer any separation between us and our Lord or between His Kingdom and the earth. We can walk and talk with Him, dine with Him, and we can let His atmosphere penetrate our being and bring life and strength to our spirit, soul, and body. If He truly abides in you, you only need to recognize He's there with you to spend time with you whenever you want to spend time with Him.

I believe every one of us can have a garden experience like I did. First, you must create a place, a specific place, in your home to get alone with God. Matthew 6:6 says, "But whenever you pray, go into your innermost chamber and be alone with Father God, praying to him in secret. And your Father, who sees all you do, will reward you openly" (TPT). You must approach Him in worship and with no agenda. My Papaw Norvel always says, "Only after you worship and praise God do you have a right to ask Him for anything." You will have to set aside time for Him; don't turn it into a religious ritual of some sort, but spend as much time with Him as possible each day. Think about it this way: if you want to be close to a person, your child, your wife, your best friend, you have to spend a lot of time with them to truly know them, to become intimate, and it's exactly the same way with your heavenly Father. Investing time with Him will get you a far greater return than any moment you spend doing something else.

The next thing you will have to do is also the hardest thing. You will have to wage war with your own mind. Joyce

Meyer calls it "The Battlefield of the Mind" because that is where the devil comes to battle us first and where we must be able to defeat him, but it is not always obvious that it is him. In other words, he doesn't usually start off with a blatant attack but with something simply to distract you. He wants to break your focus from God and woo you out from your secret place. It is not always evil things; it can just be a reminder of your "to do list," like what groceries you need for dinner that night, your child's dentist appointment the next day, or the fact your car is due for an oil change. You have to recognize the tricks of the enemy and learn to bring your mind back into alignment with God, and you must be able to lay down everything else to have that true "alone time" with Him. Talk to yourself, to your own mind, and tell it to be quiet so you can hear your Father speaking.

In the garden I visited, something very important that the Lord wanted me to see and understand was the root system. He explained how everything led back to the river and how there was more than enough food and water for all to have plenty for a complete life. There is so much power in the revelation that His life-giving nutrients are limitless. There is no competition for life, for love, or for anything else needed by the trees, the grass, or the flowers, and it's the same for us as the seed and heirs of God. Everything we could ever want or need comes from the Father. In our earthly families, sometimes we give preference to the firstborn child, or sometimes the baby of the family is given more attention, but it is not like that in the Kingdom of God. We are all His kids and we all have equal access to Him and His gifts.

If it seems some people are strong and some are weak, it's only because they have chosen not to tap in to the Source at the same level. Don't buy into the lie of the enemy that some people are special or have a greater call of God on their lives than others. We receive from Him based on our degree of hunger. The hungrier we are, the more we can learn, the more we can understand, the more power we can draw from Him. That is why the enemy does everything in his power to keep you from finding all that the Lord wants for you. If the enemy can distract you, he can dilute your hunger level for the things of God and make you less effective for the Kingdom; but we have complete control over what we draw from God's root system by how much time we spend with Him, how diligently we pursue Him, and by being a student of His Word and of Holy Spirit.

During my time in the garden the Lord spoke to me and said He is gathering all things in Heaven and earth to Himself. As He spoke, I knew Ephesians 1:10 talked about gathering all things in unity unto Him, so after this encounter I read the whole chapter. Ephesians 1:7-10 says:

> *In Him we have redemption through His blood, the forgiveness of sins, according to the riches of His grace which He made to abound toward us in all wisdom and prudence, having made known to us the mystery of His will, according to His good pleasure which He purposed in Himself, that in the dispensation of the fullness of the times He might gather together in one all things in Christ, both which are in heaven and which are on earth—in Him.*

I believe that we are in the hour when He is increasing our wisdom and understanding to make the "mystery of His will" clear to us. It's time for us to be knowers of Him and His Kingdom, according to His good pleasure. I believe we are the ones who are in this unique place in history, near the "fullness of the times," and He is gathering all things in Heaven and on earth together to Himself. *The Passion Translation* of that last verse says He is making all things in Heaven and the earth new; it is so exciting to be a part of any new thing God is doing! I know we as His children are being gathered to Him because He wants to be closer to us. He is calling us to come up higher and to walk with Him on a different plane. I also know that He is gathering lost people to reveal Himself to them in these last days.

PRAYER: WORSHIP FOR A FEW MINUTES AND THEN WHEN YOU'RE READY, BEGIN TO PRAY:

Father, here I am. I have created a place in my life to come to You, to be with You in Your inner chamber. I know I am in need of You in all areas of my life. Come walk with me and teach me how to enter Your garden and how to rest in Your most Holy place. Help me to shut down my mind, body, and emotions so that all that I am can be in that true intimacy with You. I am desperate to find my home in You and allow Yours to be in me. Come give me Your heart; breathe Yourself into me and the depths of my being. I give You permission to check my motives, to purify and burn out anything that is not of You, and to wash me in Your precious blood. I pray that Your Word comes alive inside of me as I spend time in Your presence. Take me to that place where we can walk together in all things, where You can teach me the lifestyle of holiness that pleases You. Today, I fall into Your arms longing for that touch that no man or woman can give, for Your comfort, and for Your peace that passes all understanding. All that I am wants all of You! Amen.

Now stay still before Him and wait for Him to begin talking with you. He will take over from there.

Chapter 4

Port

INVASION

O n November 1, 2016, I awoke and, as I stirred and got out of bed, I saw the clock. Again, it said 5:57 a.m., so I knew immediately the Lord was going to tell me something. However, I was also aware that there was an evil spirit in my room. I said out loud, "No sir, you're not welcome here!" and began to call on the name of Jesus. Suddenly the presence of angels arrived and I knew everything else was gone. I began worshiping and the sweet presence of Holy Spirit was very thick in the room. As I laid back down and closed my eyes, I was immediately with my angel looking over the enemy's meeting room, which was empty, and the table was different this time. It was the same color, but the parts of the frame where the legs and the tabletop joined were globes. I asked my angel, "What table is this?" and he said, "This is the table they gather at to discuss cities and nations."

As soon as he said that, the evil army entered the room from the left side, again in order, without any words to each other. They were being led by the older demonic spirit that was carrying a large rolled-up map. Following him was D with his hands full of maps as well. As they all came in both Boss and D opened and placed the maps on the table. As they did, the first map I could see was the United States. They began to talk about the borders along the waterways. As they spoke, I knew it was from the perspective that Donald Trump might be in the White House. As soon as I realized that was what they were planning for, my angel told me that it was because of all the conversations that Trump had been having about securing the natural borders. He said, "The enemy is plotting how to enter through the waterway borders and they are bringing in higher ranking spirits from other regions."

We listened closely, and they spoke of Miami, New Orleans, and a port in Maine. They were talking about bringing in demons from China and India. The spirit they spoke of from India was a sexual goddess and they discussed how it was an atmospheric spirit that affects the human desire for touch and makes the flesh crave the wrong type of touch (I believe what they were describing was like the effects of the drug X or ecstasy). My angel turned to me and said, "He will turn this all around for His glory," and he started telling me about a move of God that was coming to India. He told me that because they have been under this type of spirit for so many years, it is so easy for Holy Spirit to come in and move. He said that the people will turn their desire toward the sweet, tender, and pure presence of the Lord because when the freedom comes it's easy for them to enjoy.

After our conversation, we turned our attention back to the meeting. They were discussing something that was rising up in Kentucky and that some of the government officials there are Christians and are asking the Lord to have His way in that region. They spoke specifically of Frankfort, Kentucky (I had no idea that was the capital city of Kentucky until I looked it up the next day) and how they could release an attack to counteract this hunger of the leaders. D looked at Boss and said, "What do you think is coming?"

Boss turned and said, "I am not sure."

Before he could finish his sentence a smaller, lower ranking spirit said, "I know how to find out. I can sit at the table of the prophets and report back." As soon as he said that D and Boss both nodded their heads and that small spirit ran out the door to go to his assignment.

Then Boss and D were looking over what looked like a score card and Boss said, "As we come to the end of this thing we are winning."

They were all very proud of this score card, but then my angel said to me, "Because there is no truth in them, they have no clue that they will lose this thing," and I knew he meant the election. I was a little puzzled when he said that so he further explained that because there is no ability for them to receive truth they actually think they are winning even though they aren't. He gave me the example of when

I pray and come against the enemy and I say, "I rebuke you and I cast you back to the lake of fire you came from," and he told me they have no knowledge that there is a lake of fire that is for them. They can't hear or even understand truth because they are the product of the father of lies. He reminded me of John 8:44:

> *You are of your father the devil, and the desires of your father you want to do. He was a murderer from the beginning, and does not stand in the truth, because there is no truth in him. When he speaks a lie, he speaks from his own resources, for he is a liar and the father of it.*

Next, he explained to me about the belt of truth and that the reason it is a belt is that it surrounds the center of who we are—our bellies, where the Spirit of God lives in us. He explained that it's like it is attached by a cord to the Holy Spirit and it feeds our spirit man the truth, so we can tap on that belt any time we need truth on a matter. He began to teach me that there is a gift of truth, and that the Lord wants us to release the Spirit of truth in the last days so that eyes can be opened because when truth comes on the scene it changes everything. He said, "You must release truth in this hour to the people," and I said, "I will and I will tell others of this."

He smiled and we looked back at the meeting, where they appeared to be in meditation or something. No sound or conversation was coming out of them. I looked at my angel to question it and he said, "It is the saints."

As soon as he said that we were over a group of people praying and weeping in a living room. I did not know who they were, but I saw many angels in the room with them rejoicing at what they were doing. There was a pathway of light that was coming from behind where we were and on the path were angels coming and going, taking messages from the room and bringing messages back to the people. You could feel the angels were excited about the hunger of the people. I asked my angel, "Why are the angels so excited?"

He said, "When they see hunger they know things will start happening and begin to spread to others." He spoke of the power of hunger as if it was a tangible thing I could reach out and grab.

We continued to watch what was happening in the home and the people were crying and weeping for the sins of the nation and for the sins they had committed themselves. As they cried and prayed a cloud began to settle on the home and on the people. The people started to be more silent and still in this new Presence, and as they honored the glory of God that had entered the room, something began to happen to them. You could see they began to change in their physical bodies as well as the spiritual realm. It was like a pure glow was coming from them and they even looked younger. I turned to my angel and he looked back at me and said, "When the Presence comes like this it restores the body and will cause His glory to come reside in you."

He explained that there are different levels of the glory cloud you can enter. He reminded me of Moses and the bright glow coming from him after his encounter with the Lord and he asked, "Why do you think people (today) don't hunger to know Him more?" When he asked that it hit me in the gut. I was shocked and I realized that we can have that type of encounter with the Lord too, but I have not known anyone who has pursued Him enough to know Him like that (in other words, I haven't seen anyone walking around glowing with the glory of God). My angel said, "Know Him even more than that," and with that I was back in my bed.

Have you ever been awakened out of a deep sleep and known there was not a good presence in the room, even something evil? Immediately fear tries to grip you and I have at times frozen like a scared child until I could mumble out the name of Jesus. The enemy is very sly; he wants to puff himself up to appear to be something more powerful than he is. The first thing to remember is that He who is in you is greater than he who is in the world. All it takes is a whisper of the name of Jesus and everything else has to bow its knee to that name.

The issue is that many people allow or even invite demons into their lives, usually without knowing it. They have not allowed Holy Spirit to teach them in this area so they don't even recognize when they are entertaining the enemy in their own homes. We need to stay in a place where we are walking with Jesus, to allow Him to speak to us and walk this life out with His holiness and righteousness. The enemy wants you to be too busy to invest in your walk with the Lord and to keep you from people who have received revelation and can teach you about these things. Dr. Norvel always told me, "Be around people who know more about God than you do," and I have found this advice to be life changing for me and my family! You have to be aware of what is in your home, what movies you are watching, what music you are listening to, and so on. These are just a few things that can open your home up to allow a tormenting spirit to come in and harass you but, if you ask Him to, Holy Spirit will reveal to you the open door so you can shut it and then tell the devil to leave you alone!

This time over the meeting room, I knew there was more confidence in the enemy's team than before. They had a posture of strength, and they are proud of their plots and their plans. Even if they were not too successful with one plan, they always have a back-up plan. The power of their organization is the thing they rely on the most. I believe that they see our lack of unity in the body of Christ and they learn from our mistakes and use it against us.

Be reminded that they are not powerful unless you give them power. If you give them an inch they will take you miles down a road that you never imagined you could even be on. Think about this—when someone asks a child what they want to be when they grow up, have you ever heard the child answer, "I want to be a drug addict" or "I would love to be a prostitute"? Of course not, so how do we as people get to such extreme places sometimes? The enemy starts a person down the wrong path with one small choice, one they probably don't recognize as bad or so minor that they think they will just do it that one time and never again. But that one choice leads to more bad choices. Then, those bad choices lead to lies to hide those bad choices as they go further and further toward destruction.

Satan is very crafty so he never shows you the end result of where you are heading. This is why the Bible says to be quick to repent and turn from sin. That means a complete turn. So many times we want to repent but keep one foot in the sin and think we can get away with that with God. He says to "Be holy, for I am holy." That doesn't mean He expects us to be perfect, but to live in a way that represents Him well and to seek Him constantly, because the closer we get to Him we want less and less of anything the enemy can tempt us with.

I believe one of the things the Lord taught me in this experience was how they plot things out years in advance to attain a particular goal. "Boss" was bold in a way that he knew what he wanted in certain situations and it was his to have if planned correctly. I was surprised that they had a plan for who was going to be president, even though they thought they were winning right up until the end. This was before the 2016 election had taken place, but they were speaking of contingencies for what to do if Donald Trump was in office. Initially, if I wouldn't have known better, I would have thought they knew the future in some way, but then I was shown how they send a lower ranking spirit to sit at the table of some prophets to eavesdrop on their conversations. It also dropped in my mind the next day they have the same access we do to social media or websites that we post on, newspapers, magazines, and even books, so everything that is discussed out of our mouths they hear, then twist it and try to use it to harm us.

This is not a new trick; they've been doing it for years. They try to reproduce everything God created, add a demonic spin on it, and then release it to us. The devil even tried to trick Jesus with His own Word! This is why Jesus only said and did what His Father told Him to do and nothing more.

If you are a prophet or operate in the prophetic realm at all, you should be extremely careful *what* you release and *when* you release it so people hear it in the Lord's perfect timing. We don't want the devil to know what Holy Spirit is doing until He does it, and he can't read our minds so he only knows what we say!

As the demons discussed the borders and bringing in spirits from other countries, I learned that they are not allowed to access us without an open way in. They were discussing the natural borders, but this is about openings in the spirit realm as well. This was something I had never been taught before and, as I questioned the Lord about it in prayer in the days following, the Lord showed me in scripture that in the book of Job the enemy was not allowed to cross the land that Job owned until he was given permission. Satan had to ask to be allowed to touch Job and his belongings and family (see Job 1:9 - 2:10).

He also reminded me of how the Israelites were not allowed to enter into the promised land with certain sins because those sins have demonic spirits directly attached to them and He would not allow those demons in. He also knew if they went in too early, they would have intermarried into other demonic cultures. Those spirits went back to the curse spoken by Noah over his son, Ham, and his grandson, Canaan (see Gen. 9:22-27), and even after hundreds of years they were why God told Moses to completely eradicate the Canaanites and all the other nations around them when they took the land (see Deut. 7:1-6). They were a special people, separated from the rest of the world. Even the 400 years of slavery in Egypt was to solidify them as their own nation, which God told Abram would happen in Genesis 15:13. Because the nation of Egypt is a type and shadow of the world or flesh nature in the Bible, they had to come out from that nation both physically and symbolically and the wilderness experience was to complete that process of ridding them of those ungodly ways. An entire generation had to pass away in that wilderness just because of their sin of disobedience.

The last example He gave me was the garden of Eden. After sin came on the earth, no man or woman was allowed into the garden again and he placed angels to guard it (see Gen. 3:23-24). I understood from all this that there are definitely limits to the reach of these demons and the people with wrong motives who may bring them in. When we open doors to the enemy, we give him permission to come into our lives, our cities, or our countries, just like God gave him permission to attack Job; but we can just as easily revoke that permission through prayer and using our authority to resist him.

They were plotting to bring demons that have been given access and authority in other nations and have them sneak into the United States. I am not surprised that they were attempting this but I am surprised that the body of Christ as a whole is not even aware of the importance of keeping our gates closed. These are not just physical gates, but our eye gates and ear gates as well; we must slam shut and keep closed any little crack for the enemy to try to come in.

I think I should note here that I am not talking about legal immigration of people from other countries. I believe God wants America to continue to be a place of safety and refuge for those who are persecuted for the cause of Christ in other nations and those who want a better life and opportunities, but we must use wisdom in who we allow in so that the enemy cannot just run around unchecked.

As the demons discussed the regions of India and China, it felt as though they were proud of what they had accomplished in those nations. I looked up the sexual spirit they talked about from India and she was called Rati. She was the female counterpart of the Indian god Kama and that entire portion of their culture and mythology is tied to sexual sin and immorality. Most humans crave physical touch, and God created us to enjoy the pleasure we receive from that most intimate type of touch within the bonds of marriage, but again the devil found ways to pervert those desires. He has tricked our society as a whole to believe that sex outside of marriage is okay and perfectly normal, and more recently he has used drugs like ecstasy to mimic the effects of touch that should only be between a husband and wife, making people who use that drug even more addicted to the wrong kind of sexual contact. A direct line can be drawn demonically between those drugs and those ancient sexual spirits.

Even as I was seeing this discussion and began thinking about how this might all happen, the angel of the Lord reminded me that God will turn every attack of the enemy around for our good in some way. Because so many have fallen prey to this specific strategy of the devil and so many have been hurt by the perverted version of physical touch, it will be that much easier for God to save them when they experience the pure, loving touch of Holy Spirit. They may go so far down the wrong road that they have no choice but to turn to Him, and then He will be able to use the power of that testimony to reach many others.

I thought about my own journey and how some of my experiences led me right back into the arms of my loving Savior. Once you encounter Him and His love you never want it from anywhere else. He wants us to have that bridal relationship and live in intimacy with Him so nothing the enemy can use to deceive us is nearly as attractive as being in His arms. There is truly no other touch like it.

When the angel began to talk about the move of God that was about to unfold in the nation of India, I could hear the excitement in his voice. He talked about how susceptible they will be to the real touch of Holy Spirit. I believe that, not only in India but across the world, we will see the Spirit of God come down like rain in ways we have never seen. People's physical bodies will tremble in the presence of their Creator, and it will be a touch that they will not be able to deny is the Lord Jesus. We need to pray for that type of manifestation and make plans for teaching and discipleship that will be needed after such a mass deliverance.

I know the most important thing I was to take from this particular encounter was the power of the prayer and hunger of the saints. In the last chapter I talked about what we receive from God being totally dependent on our level of hunger, on how much we want to draw from Him because His supply is limitless. In this season, we have to desire Him like never before. Our hunger must be unquenchable, and the more we taste of God, the more we will want. Just like Solomon asked for wisdom and it was granted to him, we can ask for more hunger for the things of God and He will give it to us. He wants so much for us to experience the "meat" of who He is, the full reality of Him; and the deeper we go, the more He will reveal to us.

It was amazing to see how active and excited the angels were about how intensely the people were seeking God. They knew that the prayer of the saints was affecting the atmosphere and shaking up the enemy's camp. If we can get a revelation of the spirit realm, we can see that the angelic forces are just as real and active as the demonic forces. We have the authority to move the angels, to send them back and forth from Heaven to bring us what we need to combat the enemy and his attacks, and those same prayers can freeze the demonic forces and make them ineffective.

The people I saw were not just praying, they were desperate for God. Their physical bodies were reflecting God touching them in a real and tangible way. I could see the glow of His glory on them and my angel reminded me of Moses on the mountain. How incredible would it be to walk around with that level of the presence of God on our lives, but the angel told me we have to hunger for even more. We have to pursue Him with everything we have and everything we are. We can never be satisfied!

CHAPTER 5

Jezebel's EVICTION

O n the morning of November 9, 2016, the angel came again and took me above a large building where there was a congregation of Christians. They were all rejoicing and clapping and hugging. Then, where the balcony area was, a group of evil spirits walked in and divided the people into two groups, which caused them to start fighting with each other. That lasted for a few minutes and then people on each side started to disagree with the other people on their respective sides and those people came together in the middle and began to hug.

As they reconciled a group of angels came in and walked among the people on both sides. Some of the people recognized that the angels were there and were touched and came back to the center, but others were so caught up in their own arguments and opinions they didn't even notice the angels and didn't move. The group in the middle began to increase in size but the outer groups were still larger. The angels formed a circle around the center group and began singing, "Your Redeemer lives, Your Redeemer comes, Your Redeemer's here." The people in the center were worshiping and joyful. My angel said, "You have to be quick to hear the sound of the angels."

Then we were over a city and I could see into all the church buildings and how the people were divided within the churches. The angels I had seen earlier came into each church, and I saw the same process repeated as they tried to unite the "sides" within the churches. As I was watching this, my angel said, "The church has been divided and this is their last opportunity to come together in unity. Those who unify will experience the redemption of the Lord. To do this, they must put down their own causes and opinions. Their own voices have been so loud they couldn't hear the angels around them. They are yelling about their agendas, and some of them are even right, but because they are doing it in the wrong spirit, their own voice and opinion have become their idols. They must repent and turn away from those idols or they won't see the goodness of God or the restoration of what the enemy has stolen."

I asked him, "How long will this restoration last?" He answered, "We don't operate in time as you understand it, but in seasons."

After that, I saw that the angel, Michael, had released warrior angels who were going through the cities gathering certain evil spirits, handcuffing or restraining them, and placing them in a cage. I asked my angel, "Why aren't they being sent back to hell?" and he said, "The Lord wants them to watch. During this season those spirits will not be allowed to function on the earth."

Then I knew I was over Washington, D.C. and the White House and Michael was standing with a company of angels on the porches. He sent one of the angels inside the White House with a piece of paper and I asked my angel what it said. He answered, "It is an eviction notice for Jazz." The angel handed the note to Jazz, who looked weaker than I had ever seen before, and it was so angry it began throwing things up against the wall and outside on the lawn and her minions were mimicking her and doing the same thing.

Next we were over another gathering of people that was a different group than I had seen before. In this group everyone was worshiping and praying. I asked my angel why this group wasn't divided and he said, "This is the unified body." All of a sudden, angels appeared carrying gifts from the Father, things like the salvation of family members, an increase of knowledge and wisdom, and a revelation of the Father's love, and they also began returning things to the people that the enemy had stolen from them. After all the things had been returned, the atmosphere changed and a haziness appeared that covered this entire body of people, and then as my angel took me higher I could see that the haze covered the whole earth. I knew it was God's sweet presence and I asked my angel, "How can people reject Him if His presence is covering the whole earth?"

He replied, "They are numb. They are in a state where they can't feel or see His presence." He described it further by using the analogy of a temperature change, like when it's warm inside and cold outside, but if you leave your house you don't even sense the temperature difference. He said, "After the Redeemer comes, the next wave will be manifestations of signs and wonders. You can't have restoration or healing without Him. Every time there is a miracle, there was first a hope and a redemption. Then the healing manifested."

When he said those words, I could hear the sound of singing coming from Heaven, a song of thankfulness for redemption. It was like the sound of a party. Then he said, "It is vital that we don't suppress Him in this hour. In the past when He has given someone a word of knowledge or something to deliver, there has been a grace and plenty of time to deliver it, but that is no longer the case. When He speaks, release it immediately and with power and authority." Then he smiled at me and I was back in my bed.

I talked in Chapter 2 about the defeat of Jezebel, and in this encounter her formal "eviction" from the White House was ordered. This was symbolic of the defeat of the Jezebel spirit at the highest levels of national and even worldwide leadership because of the intensity of the prayers and declarations of the people of God against it recently. Jazz's reaction of anger and violence, and the similar reactions of all the smaller spirits that followed, is what we have seen in the natural realm with people who have not gotten their way when it comes to political and social agendas.

Sometimes we do not have the full picture of what God's plan is for a nation and why certain people gain the favor of the Lord on their lives and are allowed into positions of leadership and authority. Who are we to say whom He anoints or favors? So many times we fall into a trap when the enemy whispers to us that we have a right to judge someone else's life or their past, to disqualify them for the assignment that God is moving them into. When we allow that, even if it is just in our own hearts and minds, we have just aligned ourselves with the wrong spirit and opened a door for the demonic to come against us and judge us like we have judged others.

Since its "eviction," the freedom that the spirit of Jezebel had across the country has greatly diminished. For those of you who have fought with this spirit personally or within your family or church, you can take the authority of the blood of Jesus and evict it and cast it out from every place it has tried to take over or destroy. It may throw a fit and act like it doesn't have to leave, but just laugh and tell it to *go*. Jezebel has no authority unless you have given it a bed to lay in; so if you still feel buffeted by that spirit, you should perhaps consider going to someone for prayer and deliverance through the power of agreement.

I hope it jumps out at you like it did me how the congregation was hugging each other and rejoicing together before the enemy came in to divide them. That is God's heart for His people, but there has been an attack of disunity bombarding the church for years. It may start as just a simple disagreement that grows out of proportion. I have heard of church splits over the color of the carpet! It is crazy how easily the enemy divides us in the family of God and how this is a plot that we fall for so many times. We have to start recognizing this type of common attack and stop it before it gets any traction. Any delay in realizing what Satan is doing will allow him to get a foothold, and we can unknowingly come into partnership or agreement with those wrong spirits. The enemy will then use that agreement to bring confusion and division, dismantle your relationships, and bring hurt, pain, and destruction to you and those you were once in unity with.

As I am writing this section of the book, some time has passed since I had this encounter and I have seen such an onslaught of the devil in this area, causing people to fight and really to hate each other for no good reason other than differing opinions. In the world and even inside the body of Christ, the hatred and vitriol that people have toward others who don't share their point of view is at an all-time high.

The enemy is such a schemer and I am learning how he sets his plans in motion long before we see the evidence of them. He uses many different strategies against us, including some that he has learned from God Himself because God has used them against the enemy's forces in the past. Remember that the devil cannot create anything; he can only copy and pervert. One of the strategies God used in the Old Testament multiple times was to send confusion into the enemy's camp so that they turned on each other and essentially wiped themselves out so God's army would prevail. Now we see the devil using this same plan against us, causing us to fight amongst ourselves, especially in the

Christian world, so that we essentially get nothing done for the Kingdom.

It seems so simple to say and even believe, "I would never partner with the enemy to advance his kingdom and agenda against anyone," but we can all see at times where we have fallen for his slick words and his lying tongue to use us to cause hurt against another person. The Spirit of God is so grieved by how we can throw people under the bus at any given time, whether saved or unsaved. Matthew 7:1-2 says:

> *Do not judge and criticize and condemn others, so that you may not be judged and criticized and condemned yourselves. For just as you judge and criticize and condemn others, you will be judged and criticized and condemned, and in accordance with the measure you [use to] deal out to others, it will be dealt out again to you* (AMPC).

It's pretty clear that we need to leave the judging to God.

I recently had a conversation with someone, and as they continued talking they began to tell me that this one particular government leader was a "fake Christian"—that the person was not truly saved but was putting on a show to gain the votes of believers. As I stood there, I heard Holy Spirit say, "I never give insight to a man or woman about another person's heart on such matters." Only by the outward fruit of a person can we see the evidence of God in one's life. How can one judge a person to be fake if all the fruit of salvation is present?

Suddenly I heard myself ask the person, "Have you held the heart of this man in your hands?" It just came up out of me and bypassed my brain. Holy Spirit was talking through me, and He continued, "Fear the One that holds the heart and breath in the palm of His hands and concern yourself only with your own heart and your next breath." When I heard Him say that such a reverence came all over me and I was reminded of the scripture, "Don't be in fear of those who can kill only the body but not your soul. Fear only God, who is able to destroy both soul and body in hell" (Matt. 10:28 TPT). Needless to say, the person I was talking to hasn't accused anyone else of being a fake Christian to me again since.

One thing Holy Spirit reminds me of often is the power of compassion. Many people talk about the importance of having passion for people, which is great, but having true compassion is even more vital for it is the language of Heaven. Jesus Himself is the most compassionate example for all of us to see and that is one of the most important ways we are to be like Him. We are created in His image and when we are in true agreement with Jesus and His Kingdom, we can't help but be compassionate and love people at a deeper level. It's so important that Jesus named it as the second greatest commandment—to love your neighbor as yourself.

The enemy is the opposite of compassionate. Knowing and understanding the "language of the enemy" will help us to know when we are partnering with the right Spirit or the wrong spirit. It will help us immeasurably in recognizing if our behaviors are showing the fruit of the Spirit of God and manifesting His Kingdom on earth or if they are a reflection of the enemy and his kingdom. Here are a few examples of what to watch for:

- Gossip

- Selfishness (being inconsiderate of others or preferring yourself above others)

- Unkindness or no desire to be kind

- Vengefulness

- Stinginess or greed (not only with money but also with your time and talents)

- Contention

- Disunity

- Constant thoughts or actions of tearing others down to build yourself up

- Lies

- Any other action that is not one of the fruits of the Spirit

This is only a short list but a very good start to self-evaluate your own heart and thoughts.

Holy Spirit showed me a vision of the manifestation of gossip. I saw two women talking about someone else and, as the first woman opened her mouth to speak, a huge, nasty-looking snake came out of her and went directly into the other woman. It reminded me of a scene from the movie, *Raiders of the Lost Ark,* when Indiana Jones is trapped down in a pit full of snakes and they were slithering out of the mouths of the statues. It was absolutely disgusting and God used that vision to show me how ugly it is to partner with the enemy. One of the most powerful things on earth is agreement, so coming together in a spirit of witchcraft against another person is extremely dangerous.

We can use the Word to pray over ourselves to help with this. For example, Proverbs 4:23-24 says to "Keep your heart with all diligence, for out of it spring the issues of life. Put away from you a deceitful mouth, and put perverse lips far from you." Another translation of the first part of verse 23 says, "So above all, guard the affections of your heart, for they affect all that you are" (TPT).

All of the items on that list above are really issues of your heart that you must guard against. We should be constantly checking our motives and purposes so that we are speaking and acting from a place of care and compassion for others. It is that type of thought process that makes you want to stop everyone you meet and share your faith, pray for them for healing or deliverance, or just show them the love of Christ.

If you find yourself operating more in the language of the enemy, you can usually trace it back to being hurt by someone else, which could have festered and opened a door to a root of resentment or bitterness in your own heart. In reality, sometimes offense comes simply by believing the lie of the enemy and the source of your hurt could be something you imagined or assumed that was never even said or done against you. Be careful not to respond out of that hurt, or out of any thought or emotion for that matter, but always desire to function instead from the fruits of the Spirit.

Many times I have heard people, even ministers, make excuses for bad behavior for themselves or even the body of Christ as a whole. They use one reason or another for why certain people or groups of people are treated badly, as if they are lesser or not as important to God because of their lifestyles or actions. Sometimes they even use God's own Word to back up their wrong positions or try to explain why they are not more compassionate.

We need to have correct training on this topic. The Lord made it clear to me that His Word only "backs up" the truth. James 1:17 says that all good things come from the Father; so, if only good things come from Him, where does everything else come from? There are only two kingdoms, not three; there is God and there is the devil. There is a Heaven and there is a hell. You are either partnering with Jesus and His Kingdom or with the enemy and his kingdom. Sorry, but there really is no gray area. The sooner we understand that, the sooner we can make the right corrections in our lives.

Again, the key is your heart. If your heart has been broken or hurt in any way, you must allow the Creator of your heart to fully heal it. He is the only One who can do that completely. Don't look to any other thing or person to fill that void or relieve you from the pain. In Ezekiel 11:19, God says He will replace your stony heart with a heart of flesh, so He will take out any hardness or trauma and put back in what is new and fresh and strong again. Allow Holy Spirit to reveal where you might have a heart of stone and allow Him to replace it with flesh again.

Today there is little to no real fear of God on the scene in America, or in most nations for that matter. I am talking about reverence, not the scary kind of fear. It is also very sad how we have gotten so comfortable and complacent and how overly confident we have become in "*self.*" This is all part of the plot of the enemy to keep us trusting in our own strength rather than putting our full faith in the Lord. Some of us honor people above God or in place of God, but people are so easily deceived and used by the enemy.

The Webster's Dictionary definition of the word *idol* is: 1) a representation or symbol of an object of worship; a false god; 2) a likeness of something; a pretender or imposter; 3) a form or appearance visible but without substance. In this encounter, the angel told me that even a man or woman's own voice can become their idol. They love to hear themselves talk and love it even more when others start to love to hear them talk. If their motive is wrong or they have partnered with the enemy, what they say can be toxic, even if it is actually true.

I believe this is an area of error we have all fallen prey to, especially when you are in the heat of a discussion or disagreement. Have you ever stated your opinion or told a story and then, after a different or contrasting viewpoint is shared, you keep trying to argue or prove your point? Even if you are right in what you are saying, you have lost the spirit of humility and allowed a wrong spirit of arrogance or pride to attach to you. It's not worth it to "win" an argument if you cause pain or hurt to someone else because the enemy is literally speaking through you.

You see, we must realize that not all demonic activity is through obvious things like Ouija boards, psychic readings, or going to a satanic service. Sometimes it's the small foxes that spoil the vine. Yes, there are levels or ranks of demons, which I will explain in a later chapter, but anything evil is evil. Even if it's unintentional, we seem to justify bad behavior or engage with "little demons" like lying, gossip, disrespect, or even just laziness, because the enemy has somehow convinced us it isn't a big deal. We think things like, "Who gets hurt by one little white lie?" or "I can just repent of that later." Come on, wake up! Those behaviors are still demonic. It's always black and white; either we are operating in the Spirit of God, or we are operating in a wrong spirit.

The world is looking for attention and power. People are willing to do unbelievable, crazy, and even stupid things to find the attention they think they need. Have you ever been to a football game and seen that group of about four to five guys with their shirts off and the top halves of their bodies covered in spray paint? Even in below-freezing weather, they are always there, looking and hoping for just one moment to be captured by the TV cameras so they will be seen by millions of people.

There is something inside of us that makes us want to be seen, and just like everything else that God gave us, the devil twists that desire and tries to use it against us and actually mock God with it. The enemy thinks it is a joke, and he loves to rub something that God created to be pure into His face after the enemy has turned it into something evil. Of course, I'm not saying the guys in the football example are doing something evil. I'm just illustrating the "look at me" mentality.

When I see someone being rude or putting down others to elevate themselves, I know there is a gap inside them somewhere, a part of their lives that is causing them not to be fulfilled. They are trying to fill that gap with the approval of man or worldly gain instead of the things God wants to put inside them to fulfill His plan for their lives.

Again, this is where we must "come out from among them." God is not pleased when we desire fame or the spotlight for our own gain or our own purposes. He has given us gifts and talents to use for Him and His glory. He wants to show off through us to put us in a position of influence in order to win as many of the lost as we can, but for that to happen they have to see Him and not us.

When your flesh, your self, becomes your idol, you have come into agreement with the very root of sin itself. Any sin, whether small or great, can be traced back to selfishness in some form. What makes *you* happy, what makes *your* flesh feel good, putting *yourself* before others, and anything else centered on *you* can lead to engaging in sin. Walking in love, humility, and selflessness, basically any of the fruits of the Spirit, will always put others first and that is the only way we can restore unity to the body of Christ and to our nation.

The first step to unity is to make sure we are worshiping the right God and no other idol has stolen our gaze away from Him. We have to recognize Him and pursue Him for who He is. Seek Him as your Redeemer, not for His redemption; your Healer, not a healing; your Provider, not the provision. I believe the angels, who surrounded the first group of Christians who came into unity, were singing about the Redeemer because, in order to be in agreement, we as the body of Christ need first to come to a place of repentance. In the Old Testament of the Bible, God is the Redeemer bringing His people out of bondage, and in the New Testament He is the Redeemer from sin and from the curse of the law. Isaiah 48:17 says "Thus says the Lord, your Redeemer, the Holy One of Israel, 'I am the Lord your God, who teaches you to profit, who leads you in the way you should go.'"

It should be obvious that "the way you should go" is what we want, and He will lead us back into unity. The second group of people worshiping together was a picture of the way He wants us to be. It was amazing to see the angels bringing them gifts from Heaven, not because they were asking for anything, but just because the Father loves them and loves their worship so much. The gifts were priceless—not material things, but true gifts that could only come from above. He was really just answering their prayers and giving them whatever they were asking for because they were praying in such agreement, fulfilling His promise from Matthew 18:19: "Again I say to you that if two of you agree on earth concerning anything that they ask, it will be done for them by My Father in heaven." If the body of Christ only had a full realization of what they could accomplish in unity, they would not be in disagreement nearly as often.

I believe we need to go back to a repentant lifestyle to be brought back into right standing with Him. Search your heart, and if you find that you have been caught up in any of this activity—whether gossiping or judging others, and whether you are doing it to other Christians or non-believers—then you need to stop now and repent. Call on the blood of Jesus to wash you and break any agreements that you have made with these demonic spirits. Then make a decision to turn from this behavior and ask Holy Spirit to help you to never go back. Don't be prideful or haughty, and put down vain imaginations. Choose to walk in humility, in the fear of the Lord, and in the confidence of who you are in Christ.

PRAYER:

Lord, I ask You to forgive me for any division or discord I may have caused. I repent of all gossip and backbiting and anything I have said or done that was not in line with Your Word. Forgive me of selfishness and any dishonor I have shown toward others. In Jesus's name, I tear down any idols that I have built, either knowingly or unknowingly, and I put You back in Your rightful place of authority in and over my life.

I break any demonic attachments or partnerships I have entered into with any Jezebel or controlling spirits, and I refuse to participate in anything the enemy tries to use to keep the body of Christ from coming into true unity. Deliver me from any temptation to judge and to speak or even think negatively about others. Help me to honor not only those who are easy to honor, but also those who may not seem to deserve it. God, I ask that You remind me daily what it truly means to love my neighbor as myself and help me to treat everyone the way I want to be treated, even when they don't do the same. Help me to stay humble, yet confident in what You've called me to do.

Holy Spirit, cover the earth and bring unity back to the church. Give us the understanding and revelation of how much more we can accomplish for the Kingdom when we are all in one accord, with a focus on ministering to others instead of a focus on ourselves.

Jesus, I thank You and worship You for who You are, not what You can do for me. I recognize You as my Redeemer, my Savior, and my Lord, and I ask You to lead me today and every day into the way I should go, into Your perfect will for my life. I love You, Jesus.

Amen.

CHAPTER 6

Atmospheric
WARFARE

My angel came into my room again on November 30, 2016 and took my hand, and for the first time he introduced himself by saying, "My name is Caleb." As he did, joy completely filled every part of my heart. In the next moment, Caleb and I were above the earth looking down. I could see the enormous fires in the earth and there were spirits circling them. The smell coming up from the earth was like burnt flesh, but I did not recognize the spirits. They were dancing around each of the fires and blowing on them.

Above Israel I saw a large figure wearing a flowing white cape; the cape was exquisite and beautiful to look at and it seemed to shimmer as it reflected the light. As this being moved around, I could not see its face at first because I was not close enough. Honestly, I did not want to get any closer as this was the most demonic presence I had ever seen or come close to. Caleb turned to me and said, "That is the prince of the air, or as we call him, 'the enemy.' He calls himself 'I am' or 'lord.'" Then I heard Satan start to sing about himself and that's exactly what he was calling himself. The other spirits would continually worship him, calling him beautiful and puffing him up in every way. I was so grieved and it was almost more than I could bear to even watch them. I said to Caleb, "We need to go," but he turned and said, "No, there is a message that must be told, a warning that must be released into the earth."

Our attention went back to the scene before us, and now the enemy was giving orders to the lesser spirits about the fires and how to cause even more destruction. With every order, he would laugh sickeningly and it was the most awful sound I had ever heard. It would send demonic shock waves into the atmosphere. As he moved there was a sound coming out of him, permeating from inside him, that took on a visible form and would bounce into the air and fall onto cities or on anything that was near him. The best way I can describe it is that it looked like thick pollution. Then, all of a sudden, he knew I was there.

He came over to stand in front of us, and as soon as I saw his face I cried out, "*Jesus!*" I was not scared by his appearance itself. In fact, if it had been a normal man I would have described him as being handsome, but the overwhelming grotesque demonic and evil presence could be felt in every fiber of my being. *Repulsive* is not a strong enough word. When I screamed, Michael appeared and I stood behind him as the enemy spoke to me. I did not look at him as he spoke; I just kept my head down and closed my eyes.

The enemy began to sing another song, and the best way I can describe this song was that it had a similar feel and melody to the song "He Is" by Aaron Jeoffrey. He was indescribably prideful as he sang, "I am that I am. I am the snake in the garden. I am the murderer of Abel. I am the mob against Noah. I am the lust of Sodom. I am the doubt and fear of Sarah. I am the jealousy of Esau. I am the liar in Laban. I am the jealousy of the brothers of Joseph. I am the famine. I am the murderer of the Hebrew babies in Egypt. I am the keeper of the Israelite slaves. I am the pride of Pharaoh. I am the murmurer and complainer in the wilderness. I am the golden calf. I am the giant and the fear that keeps them from taking the promised land."

Then I spoke up and said, "Enough! I don't want to hear anymore!" but he only skipped ahead to a part about Jesus and sang, "I am the thorns in the crown on His head. I am the whip that tore His flesh. I am the spit of the soldiers on His body. I am the nails in His hands. I am His death."

I absolutely could not listen anymore, so I yelled with a loud voice and tears in my eyes, "*Enough!*"

The next thing I knew I was back in my bedroom. It was 2:53 a.m., and I was extremely shaken. I got up out of my bed and prayed and worshiped until I could get peace in my heart and spirit. I told Caleb, who had remained present the whole time, "I do not want to go back and hear anymore," but he only replied, "There is a war going on and you must sound the alarm!"

Then the presence of Holy Spirit filled my room, and Holy Spirit spoke directly to me. "Where is the prayer now? Where is the cry for righteousness? Silence and rejoicing for the victory in the election is all I hear. We are in a greater war now than we were before the elections. This is not the hour to rest and come out of your prayer closets. Gather in His name and pray, worship, and declare the works of the Lord in the land. Prophesy that the King of Glory has arrived, and advance toward the Kingdom as it advances toward you. The shift is Heaven moving toward you. Prepare the way for the King of Glory in your land!"

With that word I was able to settle back down, and as I did Caleb and I were immediately back over the earth. The enemy and his team were discussing Israel and the fires that had been burning in that region over the previous days. I heard Satan tell them, "We must keep causing destruction in this hour to keep the prime minister occupied and away from Trump." It was clear that for some reason he did not want their relationship to grow. He continued by saying, "Cause the fires to suck up their resources and billions of dollars of loss. This will keep some of the visitors out of Israel, which will help keep their economy under pressure." He talked about how they had been granted permission to spread the fires both in Israel and in the U.S. because of God's judgement of the false teaching inside the body of Christ. Satan rambled on, "This is the hour for us to advance as they (the people of God) rest."

Caleb turned to me and said, "Do not let them go back to sleep. Sound the alarm. You are at war. You must bind the enemy, loose the angels, and prepare the way of the Lord." When Caleb had finished speaking, I turned around and saw many lines of people chained to each other by metal neck collars. They were being led by demonic spirits and were walking toward a ledge. Even though the people in chains were being led directly through the fires that were burning in the cities and forests, they did not appear to see the fire or even notice the destruction that was going on around them. As they walked, or really marched, I realized they were singing about being the redeemed ones. Caleb said, "They are so deceived that they have no idea what is happening to them."

At that point, Satan came back to say something to me and again I stood behind Michael. He looked at me and snarled, "I am kidney disease," which caused a rage to rise in me.

I was so empowered suddenly that I looked around Michael and directly at the enemy in his black eyes and replied, "I will destroy you." Then he pointed at me and spoke a different disease on me, but the word that he spoke bounced off of Michael and did not touch me.

Finally, I said to Caleb with a loud voice, "Take me to the river. I don't want to see any more."

When I finished speaking, I sat straight up in the bed with great pain in my body and began to pray, but my angel grabbed my hand and said, "He did not touch you." As soon as the words had left his mouth, I realized we were in the garden of Heaven walking through the roots that run in to the river. The atmosphere there acted as a healing balm to me, with an inescapable sense of peace permeating every molecule of the air. I looked to the river and saw a man standing there, and right away I knew it was Moses. He looked completely normal, tall with dark hair, tan skin, and green eyes, and looked to be in his mid-30s. I ran to him and hugged him and said, "I am Aprile," and he responded with a smile, "I know who you are."

He started talking to me about building a temple. He said that between him and the Lord he was wanting to build the temple as soon as he left Egypt. "You see," he said, "I wanted to get into the Holy of Holies, but I did not understand that where I was wasn't the place to build it. I was still learning of the stillness of His voice. If you don't follow the detailed instructions of the Lord it can be the difference between life and death. In your day it's a slow death, but in mine it was a sudden one."

I asked, "How can I learn to hear His voice so clearly?"

Moses responded by saying, "Tune your ear, train it to hear Him in every detail, and ask Holy Spirit to help you."

I smiled and simply replied with "Okay."

He continued, "You are already so close to understanding this," and then he began to teach me about the outer courts and how important it is not to rush the cleansing process. "You have to wash yourself," and then he explained, "When you are ready to step into the inner courts you must move slowly and be quiet. It's in the stillness that you get into the Holy of Holies, into the secret place." He spoke of the holy reverence and how that reverence is the key to entrance into God's presence.

Then a group of angels appeared above us and it looked like they were standing in a loft area above where Moses and Caleb and I were. They released a sound that was announcing that there was a proclamation coming. When they finished, I heard the voice of the Lord as He began to talk about the different states of America. He started speaking about hidden gems being exposed. He spoke of the water and how in it there are many gifts to the land and its people, how His eyes are even on the many things that live in this water. He spoke of the sounds that are released into Heaven from Alaska and how it pleases His ears. He said that He will be pouring out those sounds back over her and her people in this next season and finally He said, "The cloud of rain is over you (Alaska) now." As the Lord finished speaking I realized I was back in my room and the encounter had ended.

As you read that I am certain that it shook you as it did me. This was the most demonic encounter that I have had to date and that is why I won't go into as much additional description of each part of the encounter as I have in previous chapters. I would encourage you, as I did right after this encounter, to look up and research the fires that were going on during the time around November 30, 2016. The devastation was tremendous and you can easily see the finger of Satan in those tragic events.

To hear and see how Satan mocks God is the most sickening and disgusting thing, and it is beyond any description that I could give you. He loves to build himself up and his pride and arrogance cause him to brag about what he thinks he can do to us, so silence is sometimes a key to finding out the plots and plans he has against you. In other words, when he comes and lies to you with the ways he is going to attack or even kill you, just let him talk—there is no truth in him, so his lies reveal to you how to speak the exact opposite over your life. Sometimes I actually laugh at him before I kick him out. As soon as he exposes himself, just resist him and he must flee. This doesn't just work with the enemy himself, but with anyone who comes against you. Remember, James 1:19 says, "So then, my beloved brethren, let every man be swift to hear, slow to speak, slow to wrath." Don't get angry; just listen so when you speak it will be the truth.

It's exactly what he did with Jesus. Satan should have never hung Jesus on a tree for all the world to watch His death, but he did it because he loves to show off. He really thought he had won, but Satan would have never killed Jesus if he knew that it was Jesus's blood that would rescue every person from Hell, cleanse us from all sin, and allow us to have a close personal relationship with the Father. Satan might have placed Him on the cross that day, but once he showed his hand it was time for Jesus to reveal His true purpose from the beginning of time. It was the love of Jesus for all mankind that kept Him on that cross when He could have come down at any moment. Satan gave Jesus a grand stage from which He made the biggest announcement that still rings in the earth today: "*It is finished.*" Satan was defeated and he has absolutely no authority or power over us.

I should probably explain a very personal portion of the encounter here and why I was especially bold when Satan told me he was kidney disease. You see, my earthly daddy moved to Heaven in August, 2013, from kidney failure at the age of 80, after battling it for over two years. He loved Jesus and was a wonderful father and I can't wait to see him again. I was so close to my dad, and because of that I feel like it was incredibly stupid of the enemy to have said that to me and make me so mad. Up to that point I had wanted to stay behind Michael, not hiding really, but a bit timid. However, as soon as those words left his mouth, the Spirit of the Lord arose in me with great passion to want to stand up, rebuke him, and show him I was not moved by fear anymore. Again, he exposed himself and, once I recognized his tactic, I fought back!

After this encounter, I spent the next three days really seeking the Lord for more clarity. He showed me again that we as the body of Christ are so easily distracted at times and how we have become numb to the things around us. We have in some ways become tolerant and accepting of sickness, pain, and suffering. We're barely moved by the increased violence in our world. We don't speak out or stand against abortion and blatant sin. Most importantly to Him though is that we have in many ways become so distant from Him that we don't even hear Him when He speaks.

He wants this corrected in us immediately—not tomorrow or the next day, but right now. We cannot stand silent and still for even one more moment or continue to allow ourselves to be rocked to sleep by the plots of the enemy. It takes less than 20 minutes of reading or watching any news to see the work of the enemy in our world. The Lord's questions to us are, "What part do you play? Are you going to hide in a cave and wait for My return? Are you going to build shelters to try to escape from the outside world?"

There are many of us who have taken a less radical way of hiding. We are not in caves or tucked away in undisclosed locations living off the land. We are among the people hiding in plain sight, right in front of the ones who need us. We walk through the streets of our cities blind or uncaring to those who are hurting around us. We have grown cold or careless toward the neighbor across the street who might be a single mom raising her children on a small income, fighting to keep the peace in her home, and at the same time being both a mom and a dad. We pass up speaking to an elderly couple that has no family or friends stopping in to chat with them or see to their care. Meanwhile, they can barely hear or walk and have no outside assistance.

I could go on and on about different possibilities of the people who surround us and need us, or more importantly need Who we have. We go to church, we sing some songs, we listen to our pastors, and go home, but the Lord spoke to me about this strongly. His exact words to me were, "As you stand inside these walls, people are dying, broken, abused, hungry, lost, and forgotten." I began to weep as I realized I too had indeed become numb to the people around me, even as they drove their cars right past our churches while we stayed inside the walls. Don't misunderstand what He is saying. The Lord loves that we come to His house and worship and exalt His name together. He wants to visit us there to bless us and fill us up, but not for only our own benefit. He wants us to take action for those around us and share His love, His mercy, and His grace with them. Do not be an undercover Christian, hidden in your fear or distractions. Do not try to fit in and look just like the world as if you are like them. We must come out from being camouflaged in the middle of them. How are we to lead people if we are walking beside them? We must stand out, so they might see Jesus and know Him.

The enemy understands that if he can keep us from caring about and getting involved with people then we are of no effect for the Kingdom of God and he has a better chance of using us to hurt others around us with our own garbage. Many of us have allowed ourselves to hide behind pain, hurt, or our own brokenness. We have put up huge walls to protect ourselves, hoping no one will come in and hurt us again. That is exactly the strategy that the enemy has for us. As he lulls us to sleep, he sings, "Shhhh, Shhhh, Shhhh. Stay quiet and you will stay safe. Stay hidden from all those awful people out there, because you cannot trust anyone but yourself. Shhhh, Shhhh, Shhhh. Stay quiet and go to sleep now."

That's the sound he releases over wounded believers. First, we become numb from our own pain. Next, we become numb to the sound of the sweet wooing of Holy Spirit, and last, we become numb to the lost and hurting people around us. In this phase, we are in the worst place possible because we are so caught up in our own pain that we hurt others first so that we don't get hurt by anyone. We, through our victim spirit, wound everyone around us. We allow brokenness and that victim mentality to lead us so that we can protect ourselves. Without healing and deliverance, the victim always becomes the abuser, and we see this in the natural world on so many levels. People who lie, steal, cheat, and murder were often and almost always hurt deeply as children—physically, sexually, or emotionally. You can see that those who are not believers fall into the same traps that we do. For example, the son of an alcoholic man who verbally and physically assaulted his family grows up promising himself that, "I will never be like him. I will never treat people that way." Then, before the age of 20, he has already started drinking for fun. Within a few more years he is drinking to escape his problems, and his treatment of others is getting more disrespectful and more abusive every day. Without the touch of a loving God, every generation gets worse and worse.

How can we stop this pattern in our lives? How can we come out from among them? It all starts with Jesus and ends with Jesus. I know what you're thinking. "Of course, but what does that mean to me?" It means run to Him, and stay with Him. Call out for Jesus, and He will answer your cry. Partner with Heaven to see His Kingdom invade your life and the lives of people around you. Then you become a true temple of the Most High God. Everywhere you go, people will know that you are one who walks with the Father and you abide in Him and He in you!

There is a place in the Lord, an Eden per se, for all of us. I like to call it my ark. It is my safe place, where I can truly hide in Him and hear His heart beat for me. My peace comes from meeting with my sweet Father, my Creator, and the Lover of my soul, who knows all my hidden places and knows how to woo me better than any person or spirit that walks the earth. A part of getting rid of the demonic things and thoughts we have allowed in our lives is getting into the secret place with the Lord, under His shadow. It is a place where His presence and love wash over you like a river for your soul, mind, spirit, and body. In this place is complete healing, complete acceptance, and complete confidence in who He is in you and who you are in Him. This is the place where you find the details of your life and the steps to take in the right direction. This is the place where your joy is found, and where you become equipped with power and strength that is beyond what words can explain. Run to your secret place and dine with Jesus. I promise He will meet you every single time.

The key to understanding this is that there is no perfect prayer or thing you can do except to go look for Him alone. He is everything you need. If you're looking for a healing, He is the Healer. If you need love, He is Love. If you need money, He is your Provider. If you need security, He is your Protection. Whatever you may be missing, He is all of that and more. The thing is, the Lord is a gentleman. He will not jump in where He is not invited, so it is up to you to ask Him to come into every area of your life. Every single morning invite Him in to your day. You will find His will for you and your family, so that you can walk out from among the hurting world and lead an entire generation to Jesus! We have to rescue as many as we can before He returns.

PRAYER TO COME AGAINST INDIFFERENCE:

Father, I need Your touch. Just like the woman with the issue of blood pushed through the crowd for that touch, I am in need of You so desperately that I am pushing through my own emotions or lack of emotions to get to You. I know You have never left me, but sometimes I feel as if I am walking alone, disconnected from You and who You are. Come, Holy Spirit. Come close. Lord, I need Your mercy. As I turn to You, I know You turn to me. You are my rescuer, my hero, my deliverer. Forgive me for allowing the enemy to rock me to sleep, leaving me unaware of what hurts Your heart. Turn my stony heart back into a heart of flesh again, so I have Your compassion and Your love and so I can feel again. Thank You for being everything to me and teach me to never be lulled asleep again.

*Satan, the lullaby you try to sing to me, to put me to sleep, is over. Your attempt on my life is exposed! I rebuke the sound that you have sung over me and your plots against my life. **Go** from me in the name of Jesus, never to return to whisper in my ears again. I plead the blood of Jesus over my ear gates and my eye gates. I only hear the voice of my Father and I will reject the sound of any other voice! I look only to the Lord.*

Thank You, Jesus, for breathing life back into all the areas that the enemy has come to bring death, for bringing feeling and sensitivity back to where I've been numb. I receive You, Jesus, and You are welcome in all areas of my life!

CHAPTER 7

MARKED

E arly in the morning on December 9, 2016, I was taken up above the earth with Caleb and I could feel the strong presence of Holy Spirit as well. As I looked down on the earth there were two angels marking homes in various cities with red lines of some type. The angels were not exactly the same. One was a warrior, tall and strong, whose mere presence would normally be intimidating, but instead there was a total peace, the absolute absence of fear when I was around one of them. The other angel was smaller, a worshiper who carried some type of wind instrument. Caleb took me lower to one city to see exactly what they were doing, and I could see that the warrior angel was knocking on the door of someone's house. It was not a home I knew.

A man opened the door and a woman was also there; it was a husband and wife. The worship angel released a sound and the warrior angel said to the people, "Repent, for the King of Glory is at hand." Suddenly the man and wife fell on their faces and began to repent. Holy Spirit filled their home and the angels stepped back out of the doorway and shut the door. As they did, they applied a red mark over the door. I couldn't tell exactly what they used to make the mark and it didn't appear to be blood, although I believe it represented the blood of Jesus just as the blood of animals was spread on the doorposts by the Hebrews in Egypt. It was a holy moment and I understood its significance, but it's yet another example of something that can't really be described here on earth—things for which there are no earthly words.

After the angels applied the mark to that doorway, they went to the next house and knocked, and, again, a man opened the door and I saw that his wife was inside. The worship angel released a sound and the other one made the same announcement, saying, "Repent, for the King of Glory is at hand." This time, though, the man turned to his side and pointed his finger across the room toward an old statue of a cross with Jesus on it. The statue was very dusty and looked like it hadn't been touched in years.

The husband said to the angel, "We already repented and we are good." Then he went and sat down in his recliner next to his wife and neither of them gave any attention to the command of the angel.

The first angel released the sound again and the second angel said again, "Repent, for the King of Glory is at hand," but the man said again with a loud voice, "We are good!"

and pointed to the old cross again. So the angels backed out of the house and did not mark the home.

We went to another home and they repeated the process of knocking and announcing. This time the husband and wife did not even see or hear the angels. They had a black haze over their ears and eyes. The angels tried again, but still no response, so they left that home and did not mark the door. After visiting several different homes, some repented, some thought they were fine and had no need to repent, and a few more didn't move a muscle. Every time people heard but rejected the command, they all had the same old dusty cross in their houses. After we had seen every home in that city, Caleb took me back above the earth and the same angels that were marking the homes rose up with us. As we looked down we could clearly see the houses that were marked and the ones that were not marked. We could also see homes in other cities that had been marked the same way.

As soon as all the cities were finished, a flood was released down the streets and the waters were moving very rapidly. When the water reached a home with the red mark, it would rise quickly and like a tidal wave it would overtake the home. I could hear rejoicing and worshiping from the inside of the marked homes as the waters rose and I could see angels coming and going to them as well, bringing baskets of shiny things and leaving them with the people in those homes.

There was also a very bright light coming from each of the marked homes and the light reached to Heaven. It appeared to be traveling back and forth between Heaven and the homes. Then extremely bright lights would come up from certain cities and I could hear a sound coming from those cities. The nature of each sound was quite unique and no two cities' sounds were alike.

As this happened angels appeared everywhere; thousands of them were being released into the homes where the people had rejected the call for repentance. These angels were clearing the haze that was over those people and you could see families waiting outside of the homes of those lost souls. As the angels cleared the haze, the people inside the homes would run out and cry and rejoice and hug their loved ones. Then the angels would gather around the families and then lift a banner over them with different declarations. At that moment I heard Holy Spirit say, "This is the sound of the latter rain," and I said, "I hear it, I hear it!" He said, "We are at hand." I had tears running down my face and I knew exactly what He was saying. He was speaking of Himself, Jesus, and God the Father; and He meant it is time for the greatest outpouring the entire body of Christ has ever witnessed. I was standing there with confidence but trembling in the presence of Holy Spirit.

Then He began to talk to me about the people with the dusty old crosses in their homes and He said, "They think they know." He quoted Romans 1:19-23:

In reality, the truth of God is known instinctively, for God has embedded this knowledge inside every human heart. Opposition to truth cannot be excused on the basis of ignorance, because from the creation of the world, the invisible qualities of God's nature have been made visible, such as his eternal power and transcendence. He has made his wonderful attributes easily perceived, for seeing the visible makes us understand the invisible. So then, this leaves everyone without excuse.

Throughout human history the fingerprints of God were upon them, yet they refused to honor him as God or even be thankful for his kindness. Instead, they entertained corrupt and foolish thoughts about what God was like. This left them with nothing but misguided hearts, steeped in moral darkness. Although claiming to be super-intelligent, they were in fact shallow fools. For only a fool would trade the unfading splendor of the immortal God to worship the fading image of other humans, idols made to look like people, animals, birds, and even creeping reptiles! (TPT)

As He spoke I could feel such a reverence on me and the angels. With that, Caleb came over next to me and said, "We are moving further in now. You must increase your time alone with Him."

I could feel the intensity and the weight of the glory come over me when He spoke that to me and I said, "Yes, I understand." Then I said with a loud voice, "This is what it is actually all about. Nothing else matters!" Suddenly, Michael was there. He lifted up his weapon and gave a loud war cry that all the other angels joined along with.

The cry they released rattled my very being. I noticed immediately that the wind increased, the sound of the raging of the waters flowing in the cities became louder, and everything intensified. Caleb said, "You got it," and suddenly

I was looking at my clock showing 5:55 a.m. I could still feel the sweet Holy Spirit so close.

There is a lot of marking going on in the world today. Lines are being drawn on where people stand and whom they stand with or if someone is for or against something or someone. The sad thing is so many people are making judgements and putting labels on those around them based on a lot of false information, either coming from social media or the news or from other people who have believed something that they heard from somewhere else. Dr. Norvel Hayes always said, "Don't believe anything you hear and only half of what you see." When you take the time to really dig into what you believe about a person or a particular thing, you will find that most of the time you do not have complete information or have been totally misinformed.

In the season we are in right now, I believe this "marking" is at an all-time high. It certainly happened during other times in history, but the internet has made it possible now for anyone to express or shout their opinion to the entire world in a moment. It seems like people have gotten power hungry from having the ability to write a review for anything like restaurants, hotels, department stores, and even churches and/or ministries. A process that was created for people to share useful and helpful information has become a platform powerful enough to destroy a business or a person's reputation with a few strokes on a keyboard, and what is being posted can be completely false or greatly exaggerated. Would you want to go to a restaurant where someone found a bug in their salad? In reality, someone may have just gotten mad that their water glass wasn't filled up frequently enough, so they made up a nice story about that bug and posted it on Yelp.

It's even more troubling to see reviews of churches and ministries. Posts turn into discussions, which usually turn into theological debates that would do nothing but confuse an unbeliever or cause someone looking for a good church to steer away from a certain ministry because of another person's misinterpretation of something done or said in a service. Whether it's religion, politics, or any other subject, I haven't figured out yet why people so easily believe everything they read on the internet.

The point is, we are constantly surrounded by information, both real and false, and the only way we can make right decisions is by operating in a high level of discernment. We must be able to tell the difference between a warning from Holy Spirit and our flesh just wanting to believe the latest headline or social media gossip. One of the ways the enemy is causing us to be misled or confused is by the release of so much false information—overloading our minds so that we become blind to what is real and what is truth. He tries to inundate us with so many voices we don't know the voice of the Father, but Jesus teaches about this in John 10. He talks about how the enemy doesn't just come through the front door, or in other words, he doesn't come and announce himself in an obvious way because we would easily recognize that kind of attack. Instead he comes through "some other way" like a thief or robber (see John 10:1), and plants seeds of worry, anxiety, fear, etc. through the use of this false information. But then Jesus says in John 10:4-5, "and the sheep follow Him (the shepherd), for they know His voice. Yet they will by no means follow a stranger, but will flee from him, for they do not know the voice of strangers," and again in verse 27, "My sheep hear My voice, and I know them, and they follow Me." True discernment is knowing the Shepherd's voice in every situation and listening only to Him.

In this encounter the knock came at the door, and in that moment people were given a choice. Do you want to be marked by the world or marked by God? If that knock came to your door what would be your response? I want the red blood lines over my doors because the doors represent letting Him in to my whole life! We would all like to think that we are the people who would repent and welcome Holy Spirit to fill our homes and lives, but the reality is that we do not realize how we are shutting Him out from so many areas.

There is a lot to be said about the dusty statue of Jesus on the shelf. We make our plans without Him and live in a place of complacency. A.W. Tozer said, "The stiff and wooden quality about our religious lives is a result of our lack of holy desire. Complacency is a deadly foe of all spiritual growth. Acute desire must be present or there will be no manifestation of Christ to His people." However, many people don't really even know Him or talk to Him. They don't pray until they need or want something from Him.

The old statue in your life can also be a dusty Bible. Do you study God's Word? It has also been said, "The Bible is the only book whose Author is always present when one reads it." God wants us to ask Him for revelation knowledge of His Word and He will always give it. He doesn't hide anything from us, but we can't just read the Bible to read it; we must actually desire to know the Word and know Him through the Word. We have to examine our lives and make sure we don't have any dusty statues sitting around, that we haven't become numb to the Spirit trying to speak to us.

Hearing the sound that was being released over the people and their homes shook me from the inside out, causing me to tremble. One of the things that rang through me was a strong sense of His love and understanding. As the song says, "It's love so undeniable, I can hardly speak." His longing for us to come to Him also brought on a feeling of extreme reverence.

When you go through the dating or courting process and begin to feel the early stages of love, you get that "butterflies in your stomach" feeling that grows stronger the deeper in love you get. As the sound from the worship angel rang through my ears and penetrated my being, it stirred a deep feeling in my inner man that I can only refer to as an extreme case of those butterflies. It was an excitement and feeling of anticipation, like my groom was about to walk in the door to get me.

Again, it's hard to explain, but at the very same time I felt anticipation I also learned you can't encounter the true glory of God without having felt the genuine fear of God. I had such an understanding of why God had to place Moses in the cleft of the rock so He could pass by in His glory without killing Moses in the process. He wants us to know Him as Daddy but still recognize Him as the King of Kings.

The difference between the houses and the people in them is their hearts. Do their hearts lean toward Jesus or are they more in love with themselves and the world? Even in cases where people have partnered with the enemy, it does not mean that they have turned their hearts over to him; they usually don't even know they have made that partnership.

One of the ways Satan does this is to start with confusion. He loves to get your mind clouded and unfocused. Anytime you feel confused, you know immediately it is not coming from God and you need to pray and take authority over your thoughts. First Corinthians 14:33 says, "For God is not the author of confusion but of peace." In fact, one of God's names is Peace and in the midst of confusion He will always try to woo you back into focus with His love and His Peace.

Many times I have heard that God will make you uncomfortable or take you out of a place of peace to cause you to do something. Personally, the God I know does not put you in a place of discomfort or make you miserable so that you do something or to cause a change in you. Why would your Father, someone who is called Peace, push you away from Himself and into turmoil? I have found in my own life if I am in a state of discomfort it is a place that I have allowed myself to get into because of some area of disobedience, but even in the midst of the hardest times I can always find Him and His peace. I'm certainly not saying that it will always be easy or even that God doesn't allow us to be put into uncomfortable situations, but He also does not want us to be on some emotional roller coaster. Even while he was being stoned, Stephen looked up to Heaven, saw Jesus, and died in perfect peace (see Acts 7:55-56, 59). In every situation, pursue God and seek His peace that passes all understanding.

Can you imagine being caught up in a flood from Heaven and the Lord walking up and down our city streets? This is what I know is approaching the earth; we will see the tangible move (flood) of the Spirit of God come into our cities and bring all of His glory in a way that the early church talked about and, I believe, in the way they tasted of when Holy Spirit came and filled the upper room. Acts 2:2-6 says:

> *And suddenly there came a sound from heaven, as of a rushing mighty wind, and it filled the whole house where they were sitting. Then there appeared to them divided tongues, as of fire, and one sat upon each of them. And they were all filled with the Holy Spirit and began to speak with other tongues, as the Spirit gave them utterance. And there were dwelling in Jerusalem Jews, devout men, from every nation under heaven. And when this sound occurred, the multitude came together, and were confused, because everyone heard them speak in his own language.*

The key scripture there is verse 6: "And when this sound occurred." The sound that came down from Heaven into that upper room actually was heard throughout the whole city and drew people out of their homes to see what was happening and then they encountered the Holy Spirit shortly after that. People didn't know what was going on until Peter quoted Joel's prophecy: "And it shall come to pass in the last days, says God, that I will pour out of My Spirit on all flesh" (Acts 2:17).

We can only imagine what that sound was like, but I know it's coming again to the earth soon. I also know the sounds I have heard during these encounters are not earthly sounds and cannot be explained. They vibrate the inner core of a person and your inner man has no choice but to respond. Your flesh trembles as the sound draws you in. The host of Heaven is calling you to your Creator and you cannot resist; you must find the source of this sound. This same sound and Spirit will draw the unbelievers to the amazing Jesus who is calling us all to know Him more, and when we step into this flood the gifts of God are not held back from anyone!

As the angels removed the demonic haze, the air became crystal clear for everyone to see the truth, and the gathering of loved ones was so powerful. I know that there is a season coming on the earth when all darkness will be pushed back and the ones who have been bound in such demonic confusion will be able to see things more clearly and will be given a chance to return home and repent of their sins. As they turn their back on the enemy, they will fall into the arms of their Savior.

We as the body of Christ must prepare for this harvest. Teachers, get your studies completed and prepare your notes. Pastors, find your oil and tissues because as they return they will be longing for the love of the shepherds. Apostles, build the churches and prepare the way of the Lord as John the Baptist did. Prophets, tune your ear and clear your hearts for the Word of the Lord; He will need your tongue to be loosed to release life and destiny into these new believers and you will guide and direct the flow of the Holy Spirit. Evangelists, find your fields and get in them. Pray for strategic alignments to whom you can send all these babies. We must not allow the enemy to steal the seed of salvation!

There is no job greater or more important than another; we all have a massive job ahead of us. Listen closely for the instructions of Holy Spirit. If you are unsure of your position or assignment, press in to the secret place and He will always reveal His will for you and your family. Intercessors will be needed to help keep the enemy's forces at bay and we must all pray, without ceasing, with the power of the Holy Spirit. I love the power of the prayer of faith and agreement. We must have complete unity in the body for this great hour. As we prepare for this final move of God, I believe we will be protected by the cloud of glory by day and the fire of God by night.

I pray you are challenged by this chapter to make sure you have no dusty Jesus statues in your life and, if you don't know Jesus personally or are not 100 percent sure you are ready to meet Him in Heaven, I have included a "sinners' prayer" in the back of this book. It is not just saying the words that will change you, but the Bible says to confess with your mouth *and* believe in your heart and you shall be saved! Just turn yourself over to Him right now, today. He will be so excited for you to come home!

I have also included a prayer below that I believe will help us get rid of the "dust" in our lives, some of which we may not even know is there. As in previous chapters, the way I love to enter prayer is through worship. Remember, Holy Spirit is a person. He is a gentleman and He comes by our invitation. Just begin to worship the Lord, focus your mind on Jesus, silence your emotions, and let Holy Spirit draw you to Him! When you are ready begin to pray:

Jesus, I love You! Holy Spirit, I need You to search my heart and my very being, all of who I am. I invite You today to come and cleanse me, heal me, correct me, and teach me about Jesus. I want to know Him the way You know Him. Bring up anything that may be hidden in me that is not of You! Do not allow any unforgiveness or bitterness to remain in me. Do not allow disappointment or heaviness to keep me from Jesus. I want to encounter all of Heaven, all of You, Holy Spirit, and all of You, Jesus. Come walk with me and talk with me! Help me to stay hungry and thirsty for You. I long for righteousness and what is holy in Your sight. Keep my wandering eyes fixed on only You, Jesus! Do not allow any demonic haze to linger in my life that would blind or confuse me. Do not allow me to become stale and stagnant or to become unaware of dust on the Word of God in my life.

Prepare me for the harvest that is about to be released on the earth. Allow me to be in the right place at the right time; I don't want to ever miss You! Order my steps to be in Your perfect will so I can be most effective for the Kingdom of God. Align me with others who have the same laser focus on You, Jesus! Be my true Shepherd and keep me safe. Keep all evil spirits away from me and my family and protect the call of God on our lives. Allow Your voice to be my only influence. Forgive me if I have allowed wrong voices to impact my life in past situations. I lay my life down at Your feet and surrender my will, my desires, and my motives to You! I want to lose my life so I can truly find it.

Lord, keep Your blood over the doors of our lives at all times! Do not allow us to become cold or distracted! I plead the blood of Jesus right now over my home, my life, my business, my finances, my family, my friends, my church, my state, and my country! I declare I will be ready to do my part to help usher in the glory of the Lord! I open up my life and say King of Glory come in! Invade all of me! I belong to You, wholly and completely. I love You, Jesus, and in Your name I pray, amen!

CHAPTER 8

His RIVER

It was early in the morning on Christmas Day, 2016, and Caleb and I stood over the boardroom, which was empty at first. Then Boss and D came in together discussing the defeat of Jazz. They did not seem to be very upset about this, except that they had to change their future plans and plots against the body of Christ. They discussed how the body is in a state of encouragement and how easily they have overcome that before. They brought up stories of defeat and how they need to bring in something stronger this time.

Boss called in a new demon I had never seen or heard of before. When they called this new demon in, a mist filled the air as they spoke its name. They called it Zoso.

This demon appeared to be in the general form of a male human, walking on two legs and wearing a black and white leather-type outfit. He exuded an arrogance of a false god, and he came in with other smaller spirits following behind, seemingly worshiping him. These little demons reminded me of an insect I used to chase as a child that I called a "lightning bug." They had two sets of paper thin wings and their countenance seemed to be an almost iridescent green or yellow color. As Zoso spoke, the mist in the room thickened. I was taken aback by his extreme confidence and how he spoke with authority like a military leader or dictator. Even in a room of demons, his presence made the atmosphere even more evil. Boss said to him, "You have done well for us, but now it's time to release your greatest power over the anointed ones." Zoso replied with how he will use his ability to afflict people to sicken them and bring disease and pain to their bodies. Boss said, "For the ones you cannot touch, you can release pain to their mental state and to their emotions."

Boss and D began to explain to Zoso and his minions that all they needed from them was to distract "the anointed ones" with pain of any kind so they could come in with a larger attack. They discussed the different areas in people where they could cause pain—for instance, the emotional realm, physical realm, etc. Pain is their most common weapon because it causes people to be distracted enough to allow the enemy to come in with other attacks. Boss said he just needed these attacks to intensify over the next few months and Zoso replied, "Okay, I can make that happen."

A few days later, on December 29, 2016, as I was standing in front of my bathroom mirror getting ready for a business appointment, I was taken back to this same exact scene, and, after the statement above by Zoso, a strange thing happened. From the right side of the room, a stampede of elephants came in. Not only did I see them and hear them, but I could literally feel them shaking the ground and everything around them. As they ran through the room and out the left side, they went around the conference table with some on each side. This stampede lasted for what seemed like several minutes, with many, many elephants running through. I'm not sure if it is important, but all the elephants were adults; no baby elephants came through the room. Despite the huge number of elephants and the force with which they came through, there was no damage done to the room. Although the demons in the room did not speak during the stampede, they did not seem to be affected by the elephants. I got the impression that they couldn't see the elephants, but only felt the shaking and were aware something was happening. I had no fear during the stampede and I was glad the elephants were running through their room, but I was puzzled by the event and not sure what it meant. I asked Caleb to explain it to me, but he just smiled and told me to research the meaning of elephants in prophetic dreams. Instantly I was back in front of my mirror at home.

Back on Christmas Day, I turned to Caleb and asked him if we could go back to the garden and instantly we were at the bank of the river and I was leaning against one of the trees. Caleb said, "It is easy to defeat the enemy," and another angel appeared and sat down with us. I immediately knew this angel was a carrier of information, and as he spoke I felt like a student in a classroom with a professor.

He began to talk about how we defeat the enemy and started by saying, "You were created as a spirit, soul, and body. When the enemy attacks you he can only do it in the soul and the body. However, if he can keep you operating in your soulish area, he can keep your spirit man suppressed."

He continued to explain that people try to battle the enemy in their soul and in their mind, and that is why the body can start showing the outward effects of that battle. A wounded soul, an embattled soul, will actually start to manifest the damage it receives during the spiritual battle in the physical body. It is the equivalent of going into war with no armor or no protection. Then the angel quoted part of John 10:10, saying, "The enemy comes only to steal, to kill, and to destroy." He said that when a person is born again, they immediately possess joy, peace, strength, authority, and everything else good. The enemy's initial attack then is to the soul, to a person's emotional realm, to steal that joy or that peace so he can then kill your will, and once your will is gone he can destroy you.

In that moment, I was reminded of the girl in my earlier encounter who was brought in defeated and ready for the death blow until Jesus rescued her and restored her will. Then the angel said, "You have to change the order. You have to move your spirit to the front line and that is where you do battle with the enemy. Your spirit keeps your soul and body in proper alignment according to how you were designed." He told me that the body will always function according to what is happening in the soul and the soul should function according to what is happening in the spirit. He said, "That is why the enemy comes after your soulish realm so hard; he cannot get to your spirit man without overcoming your will, which lies within your soul."

As I sat there and listened to every word, I noticed that in the background there were sounds of worship that were bringing healing to me. As the sound waves were rushing over me, the angel said to me, "The sounds of Heaven will open their hearts, heal their souls, and awaken the spirit man of the lost children." When he said that I had a memory of me as a child. When my mom would want me to come home and I was running around the neighborhood with the other kids, she would release a sound. It was a unique whistle that I knew meant it was time to go home. All the neighborhood kids knew when my mom called for me because of this sound. It seemed like it could catch my ear a mile away. Then Caleb, my angel, spoke and said, "Yes, that's it," because he knew what I was thinking. I understood how important it is to release the sound of Heaven on earth.

Then the other angel said, "Let it flow from your spirit man."

I smiled and said, "Yes, I can do that."

As soon as I said that the other angel got up and said, "I have much to do, but we will talk again soon."

Caleb said, "Let's get in the river before you go back to the atmosphere of earth," so we ran and jumped in the river. As I stood there in the water, all of a sudden a rush of emotions hit me, like the understanding of where we are in the body of Christ and how thankful I was for the experiences that I had been having in the garden. Caleb said, "You must stay ready, for the enemy always tries, but remember, everything he tries will eventually fail."

With that statement I was back in my bed. As I got up on Christmas morning, the sweet Holy Spirit said, "There are many gifts for the body today."

As I began to study out the events of this encounter, the first thing I looked up was Zoso. Most of the references to this word on the internet are for a name on an old rock album, but when you dive a little further you will find the name is deeply rooted in the occult. One reference even refers to Zoso as "the beast." As this demonic spirit was introduced, I was very grieved by his confidence in his ability to play games with people and to cause them pain. We never want to partner with him to allow pain in our lives or, even worse, to be used by him to cause pain to someone else. I realized that I have certainly fallen prey to these taunts and deceptions from him, when my mind and my emotions began to lie to me in multiple areas. I also recognized situations when he had used other people around me to reinforce a lie that had at some point popped into my head.

You have to understand that the enemy wants to tempt you to take ownership of sickness or some kind of condition that is not of God. Many times when we feel an ache or pain, the devil's purpose for that is to see if you will partner with that pain and accept it. If he can get you to believe the lie that you have something wrong with you, he can actually get a foothold to attack you. There is science now that shows people have had nothing medically wrong with them, yet have become very sick just because they thought about it so much they convinced themselves of a lie. I like to use this example. When something is baking in the oven, you usually smell it way before it's done cooking, and that smell is drawing you to want to eat it. But what if you are on a diet and you walk past the bakery in the grocery store and smell all that fresh bread and see those cakes in the display case? Your first reaction is to forget the diet and eat some of those great-looking carbs, but you have to make a decision to walk away. You have to have a strong enough will to say no to that temptation. It won't hurt your diet just to smell it or see it, but it will if you buy it and eat it. It's the same way with sickness. When the enemy puts a symptom on you, you can reject it or you can own it. Just resist the devil and he will flee!

This should be common sense, but I feel like I have to say it anyway—not every idea or impression you get is the Spirit of Truth. However, discerning between what is God and what is not God is easier than you think. Again, James 1:17 tells us, "Every gift God freely gives us is good and perfect, streaming down from the Father of lights, who shines from the heavens with no hidden shadow or darkness and is never subject to change" (TPT). That's really pretty straightforward, but we usually try to make it much more complicated. If something isn't good, it isn't from God. No darkness can be in Him, no shadows, nothing evil. He is steady and does not change.

Sometimes we get so caught up in the works of binding and loosing from our own strength that we forget about letting our good, good Father take care of us. He will speak to us, warn us, and give us instructions like a GPS to avoid pitfalls and wrong directions. Then, ironically, after He tells us what's going to happen, He will actually step in and handle the situation completely for us if we will let Him. Sure, He will walk us through the fire, but isn't it better to avoid the flames altogether? Trust Him to go before you and fight your battles for you.

I love the simple truth of His Word, and it says we can cast all our cares on the Lord. Seems too good to be true, right? It is absolutely good and it is absolutely true. The enemy lies to us to get us into a place of worry, anxiety, or fear, and if we listen he will play games with our very lives. But if you find yourself struggling with that spirit of fear, just lean on Jesus and turn over every burden, because 1) He genuinely desires to take care of you, and 2) He will never leave you nor forsake you, no matter the circumstances you are in or what you did to get into those circumstances to begin with. It really is that easy; so as soon as a thought comes from the enemy, you have to take it captive and reject all negative thinking.

Of course, there is a major distinction to be made here between a demonic thought or feeling, such as pain or depression, and a check or warning from Holy Spirit when there is something to be on guard for. That is why discernment is so important. First John 4:1 says, "Beloved, do not believe every spirit, but test the spirits, whether they are of God." We must stay close to Holy Spirit and constantly seek to learn His voice so we know it when we hear it and never listen to the voice of another.

Like we discussed in the last chapter, one of the major issues in the body of Christ we are facing today is that some people are branding others with demons or spirits that may or may not be truly there, causing hurt and rejection. They are sitting in the seat of judgement with a label gun, "printing" names on people. We must remember that even when a person is dealing with demonic oppression, they are still a child of God and He wants to save them. Our job is to show them the love of Jesus and help them get deliverance so they can rise to their rightful place in the Kingdom. Holy Spirit never shows you another person's issues or demons so that you can use that information to hurt them; so if that is happening around you then you may be getting your information from the wrong spirit, or Holy Spirit wants to use you to help that person.

This is an area that God had to deal with me, and He taught me that I must clearly separate the issue or the devil from the actual person. You have to look at people through the eyes of the Spirit, not from your soulish area. Always remember the words of Paul, "For we do not wrestle against flesh and blood, but against principalities, against powers, against the rulers of the darkness of this age, against spiritual hosts of wickedness in the heavenly places" (Eph. 6:12). *The Passion Translation* says it this way, "Your hand-to-hand combat is not with human beings, but with the highest principalities and authorities operating in rebellion under the heavenly realms." We are in a war against the enemy, not people; if we don't learn to separate the two, we will leave a path of pain and destruction in others, which is the devil's ultimate plan.

One of the greatest examples of this is when Jesus was on the cross looking at those who were literally committing murder against Him, who were, even if they didn't realize it, cooperating in the spirit realm with Satan himself. Through all the pain and anguish, He still was able to separate the humans from the spirits in operation as He prayed for them, "Father, forgive them, for they don't know what they're doing" (Luke 23:34 TPT). I pray that we can have the heart of Jesus to show that type of compassion to everyone, no matter how much they hurt us, and I am eternally grateful He looked past my issues and asked the Father to forgive me anyway.

We also have to remember that the enemy can't create anything new, so we are just facing the same old demons over and over. Think about some of the terrorist organizations in the world. It was almost 30 years ago that al-Qa'ida was founded by Osama bin Laden, but when he was killed, that same demonic spirit of fear that is always looking for a new person to use to cause torment and pain to people, especially to Christians, continued in the leaders of ISIS (or ISIL).

That is an extreme example, of course, but it's the same pattern Satan uses to come into a church or ministry group and find someone else who will partner with him to gossip or bring discord. He is very focused on creating division because he knows that Jesus said in Matthew 18:19, "Again I say to you that if two of you agree on earth concerning anything that they ask, it will be done for them by My Father in heaven." The enemy knows to take that Word literally, that "anything" actually means "anything," so he is terrified of what the body of Christ can do in unity and wants to do everything in his power to keep us in disagreement. Refuse to be that person who partners with demons!

The elephants may have had several meanings, and I admit I'm still not absolutely sure why I was shown this, but here are a couple things I believe God was showing me during that "repeat visit." First, elephants represent a strong and united family unit, resembling what God wants in His own family, which is the body of Christ. A united group of believers can literally cause a stampede through the middle of the enemy's plans. Nothing can get in their way when they are all working together toward a common goal.

Elephants also represent faithfulness. They are primarily pack oriented and stay together for life, even mourning for the death of one of their members. They are a good example of how we should care for each other's feelings and yield to leaders with more age and wisdom. Dr. Norvel would often say that believers needed to be more like elephants—to have very "thick skin" to resist offense and hurt, but also have love and a deep level of tenderness toward others. We definitely must resist offense, as more than one of these encounters have shown me that is one of the first and easiest ways the enemy can get us to partner with him.

I learned so much from the "teacher" angel as he explained how vital it is for us to combat the enemy's attack in the spirit realm and not try to fight him in the natural. Satan is the ruler of the earthly kingdom, and he is stronger and smarter than us if we try to war with him in his domain, which is our flesh and soulish area. But the Bible says in First John 4:4, "He who is in you is greater than he who is in the world," so when we rely on Jesus and the Holy Spirit within us to do the fighting we can never lose. This angel explained so clearly that when we go into this battle alone, it is like going to war with no armor. The enemy can hit us with pain and hurt in our emotions, which eventually will manifest in our physical bodies if we don't fight back with the right weapons, which we know from Second Corinthians 10:4 are "not carnal but mighty in God for pulling down strongholds."

In the natural, we put so much weight on things we can see and feel but barely any weight, or none at all, on things happening in the spiritual realm, when it should be the exact opposite.

So often we get out of that proper alignment. We try to do things in our own strength and with our own understanding instead of leaning on the Spirit who has an infinite supply of both. Like Caleb said to me in this encounter, it is easy to defeat the enemy. Don't give in to the lies that living in victory is hard or a constant struggle. If your spirit man is properly aligned, your thoughts and actions and even your personal health will follow.

When we are walking and living in that correct order, we will produce a sound that will draw others to Him. It is a unique sound that people will recognize is different from the other sounds they hear on a regular basis. This sound brings peace, joy, and happiness and provokes people to jealousy of what we have inside us. They will want to be around us and hear the good news of the Gospel. We must be open and allow ourselves to be vessels He can use at any time to reach the lost.

Lord, here I am with my heart and my life open before You. Examine me and see where there are areas that I have not yet turned over to You and Your authority. Give me the understanding that You desire for me to trust You in every area of my life. Help me to see clearly when I am partnering with the devil to cause pain or destruction in my life or in others around me. Forgive me for holding on to areas that I have not trusted You in, for thinking I knew better, or just for wanting to keep my own control over some part of my life. God, I give You full permission to completely control my _____ (fill in any areas here that you have not given Him total control, for example: marriage, money, children, other relationships, bad behaviors or habits, etc.). I plead the blood of Jesus over all of these areas and I ask You, Lord, to teach me to allow Holy Spirit to take over every area of my life and lead me every day. Help me to come out from among the world so I can win as many people as I can for Your Kingdom. Holy Spirit, I give You permission to fill any parts of my heart that have turned cold or have been wounded or that for some reason I have tried to hide from Your healing power. I trust You with everything and I want to walk with You in every area of my life. I love You, Lord, and I give it all to You, for Your glory, and for Your will to be accomplished in me and through me. Amen!

CHAPTER 9

A
THIN
Line

t was January 5, 2017 and I was standing on the edge of Heaven facing toward the earth. A huge group of both people and angels was standing with me, all facing toward earth as well. There appeared to be millions in this group, stretching as far as my eyes could see to my right, to my left, and behind me. The people were the redeemed ones, the cloud of witnesses. Some of them were calling out to the earth, saying, "Come to the Father," and I knew they were speaking to those who were already believers to come closer to God. Others were calling out for healing and deliverance, and still others were releasing a sound for the harvest. The sound was not earthly, not like a cry or even a language; it was a sound from the depths of those who had full knowledge and understanding of the power of the blood of Jesus to save. They were extremely passionate and together created a very loud roar. The angels were geared up and ready to be launched into the earth's physical realm whenever the order came. Their excitement for what was being released was beyond me. The confidence in what they were about to do was so real and tangible; it was a level of faith that is not found on the earth. The only way to explain it is that they knew their work was already finished before it had even begun.

Between Heaven and the earth was a thin line. It wasn't a visible line; it was more like just a dimensional threshold of some type, but there was a definitive difference between the two atmospheres. They were so close together it felt like I could step over at any time I wanted into either one, but Heaven was constantly pulling me to come closer!

On the earth side of the line, there were also millions and millions of people as far as my natural eyes could see. However, they were not looking at us or toward Heaven at all; they did not know we were even there. They were rushing around in their busy lives. Then, all of sudden, I realized I could reach over the line and grab one. As soon as I pulled someone over to Heaven, their family would come running to them and greet them with so much love and with joy for them to be there. It is not as if they died or moved to Heaven in the way we think of it in the natural, but they had made Heaven their eternal home. Their destiny was now Heaven.

I did this a few times and then a different sound came from behind me. It sounded as if many wind instruments were playing in unison, like different types of horns, flutes, and other instruments I couldn't discern, but I could definitively hear the sound of a shofar. This continued for several minutes, and as the sound brushed over me it was so powerful my hair blew forward as if by a strong gust of wind. I realized it was the breath of God, supporting and strengthening all of us doing the work to bring as many over into His Kingdom as possible.

As this sound moved through the crowd of people and blew across the line into the earth, the people there suddenly were aware of it and turned toward Heaven. In that moment, it seemed time itself was standing still, waiting for the final sound wave to reach the farthest reaches of the planet. Then Caleb said, "There is a time coming when there will be a sound released out of Heaven into the earth that will cause the people to know Heaven is present. During that time the unbelievers may be gathered into the Kingdom and it will be the greatest harvest in history. Everything is leading to that moment."

I asked, "How can so many be saved in just a moment?" He reminded me time doesn't mean the same thing in Heaven that it does to me on earth.

He explained that, in Heaven, a moment is when something happens, not a measurement of time. Then he asked me, "Do you understand why so much preparation has been necessary before this sound can be released?" I told him I thought it was because of the multitude of people and the value of so many, and, as I answered him, I felt an intensity of love and compassion for the people.

Caleb told me I was thinking the right way and then he began to tell me that the people on earth don't comprehend how close Heaven really is to them. He said, "Even the church doesn't realize it is only a step away," and he told me I have to help get them ready. "Understanding that they are not of that world is what they must know. He sent you into the world with the Word and His truth. Jesus has placed His truth in you with His message so they will find Him! Release Heaven! Release His message so they can hear Him through you. Go into all the places He leads you; you are with a company of Heaven as you enter through. Be among them but not of them. Be Him manifested on earth!" With that I could hear the roar of the people on Heaven's side of the line again, and I could still feel their excitement and anticipation of what was coming as I realized I was back in my room.

The line between Heaven and earth is so thin in this hour that it is barely recognizable. We must realize the access we have to Heaven and the angels. All of Heaven is calling us to come up higher and join with them, and we can call Heaven down so that God's will may be done here just as it is there. I believe the line gets thinner every time we pray as Jesus taught the disciples in Matthew 6:10, "Your Kingdom come. Your will be done on earth as it is in Heaven." The veil is being lifted, removed completely really, and the angels are being prepared to be released to gather the people of God. Heaven will invade our world as we welcome all of it to come!

There is nothing Hell can do to make the "line" thicker or push Heaven away from you and your family. The only way the enemy can walk you away from Heaven is if you join hands and partner with him. Open your heart and spiritual eyes and ears to see that Heaven is your real, true residence, and let the sound of Heaven call you home not in the natural but in your spirit and soul. We must allow all of Heaven to invade our earthly beings here so we can represent Him as His ambassadors.

We need to understand the price Jesus paid was not for our earthly gain but for us to be able to access Him and the Father. It was all about restoring the relationship between God and man that was lost at the fall of Adam. A few years ago, my husband wrote a song called "Here I Am" that describes how every time we tell God we need Him He is instantly right there for us. He wants us to know how close He really is at all times, that we can reach across that "line" at any time to get to Him.

Can you hear the breath of God calling you to encounter Him? Since this experience, every time the wind begins to blow with force around me in the natural realm I love to run outside and stand in it and feel it on my skin! It is far from what I felt in that heavenly atmosphere but still a reminder of His strength and power.

His true breath is not describable but it is undeniable. You could never be confused or wonder if it was Him blowing on you. After you feel His breath and hear His sound, no one can convince you that you imagined it or it didn't really happen. No demon in hell can steal it from you. No one and no thing can remove the sound of Him from your ears because you carry Him inside you. His breath penetrates you and there is nothing like it. It is the very thing that gave you life. We must understand the power of His wind and the sound it makes. It's the sound that will be released in these last days that you must recognize and teach others to recognize as well.

How can we cause His breath or His wind to blow here on earth? That is the question that lingered with me for days after this encounter. I know that as I pulled people across the line into Heaven, His breath came and I believe that is what will cause Him to blow again on earth. Even in our churches we have lost the manifest presence of God because we have focused on the wrong thing. There is nothing wrong with bright lights and great music, but it is the body's job to add souls to the Kingdom and unless we get back to the basics we won't see His breath.

As I sought the Lord on this He began to take me to the Word in Genesis where He breathed life into Adam and Eve. There are so many faces in Heaven with so much diversity. So many different colors, shapes, and sizes, yet there is a distinct similarity in every one of them. That similarity is the actual likeness of God because we all are made in His image and we were all created by His breath. We may not look like Him in the natural, but if we are truly saved, we all look the same in the Spirit. It was by His spoken Word that He created man and all the heavens and the earth as well. The fact that He spoke those words means there was a sound that came forth and the sound must have breath to be produced and released. The breath is what pushes out the sound and carries it into the atmosphere.

Sometimes He speaks through a still, small voice and sometimes it is like booming thunder. The more of His breath He uses, the louder and more intense His words become. He used my own breath to teach me more about this. He had me start off with a whisper and get louder as I put more breath behind it. There are no words or sound at all without breath.

He told me there are so many out there with sounds, proclaiming different things about me, but it's not my sound. All things that have breath have a sound inside of them. It all depends on who is the owner of the sound. Many times we can find ourselves being distracted by the wrong sounds that are trying to woo us away from our Father. Now when I walk into different places I know that He is with me and I am looking for the opportunity to release Him in that region, looking for others who understand they are Jesus carriers, listening for a group of people who have captured the sounds of Heaven. We must partner with each other and with the Spirit to release His sound together because the more of us there are in unity, the stronger the breath and the sound that comes forth.

You need to understand that sound itself is a powerful thing. Sound waves can be used in concentration to break up other solid matter and at the right decibel level can cause harm to your physical body. Think about it—every creature was created with its own unique sound. Even the rocks were given a sound at creation, which we know because Jesus told the Pharisees in Luke 19:40 that those rocks would cry out to praise Him if the people didn't. The wind has sounds that change with the force with which it is blowing. I love the sound of a soft breeze but I have also heard what compared to the roar of a freight train as a tornado passed close by my home.

Even Satan himself was created to produce sound. Ezekiel 28:13 says, "The workmanship of your timbrels and pipes was prepared for you on the day you were created," and the word "pipes" there means wind instruments. Now he loves to use his perverted sounds to lie to us and bring confusion and manipulation, and we must learn not to listen to him.

Many of the plots against the body of Christ and the attacks that the enemy brings are to knock the breath out of you. With no breath you are weak and you have no ability to release the sound of God that is within you. The devil does not care about you unless you are advancing the Kingdom of God, so if he can take your breath you can't share Jesus with the world around you. What you have to remember is that Jesus is inside you and He is never weak or out of breath. In your home, allow Him to breathe through you. When the attacks come, allow Him to breathe through you. When someone is hurting and God tells you to minister to them, allow Him to breathe through you. His breath will bring strength and healing to every situation.

I know many of you may have lost your breath or your will to fight. During seasons of pain or dryness you must surround yourself with people who know more about God than you do. Don't allow your flesh to win. Don't be distracted by petty issues. Push through. Worship and praying in tongues must be your priority so you come into perfect alignment and agreement with Heaven over your life; and when you are in that perfect will of God, you can take joy in knowing that you are already on Heaven's side of the line.

I'm not saying it's easy all the time. Do not take your salvation lightly or for granted. Philippians 2:12 says to "work out your own salvation with fear and trembling," which means to do it with reverence and understanding of its weight and importance. Stay hungry for the Word and thirsty for the Spirit. Ask Jesus to let you drink of that living water and let it permeate you from the inside out.

The angel, Caleb, taught me so much in this short encounter. The sound is coming soon that will draw all people to Jesus and we are that sound. We know the end-time harvest is coming because the Bible tells us it is, but even though we don't know exactly what that will look like, we have to get ready and prepare for it. When God told Noah to build the ark, he had never even seen rain, let alone a boat. Yet, when he reacted in faith and obedience, he received exact dimensions and directions to accomplish God's plan. We just need to ask Holy Spirit to give us the blueprints.

I believe Caleb was just reminding me the time is now and the body of Christ must be the ones to release the sound of Jesus to as many as we can. Jesus Himself said in Luke 17:26, "And as it was in the days of Noah, so it will be also in the days of the Son of Man." He was telling the apostles that no one will know exactly when He is coming but we need to be ready and help get as many others ready as we can. Before the flood, people were just living their lives, eating and drinking, feeling like they were invincible as the world around them got more and more evil, and that is exactly the plan the enemy is repeating now.

Don't let Satan keep you from telling people about Jesus. Don't let him lie to you that you're not good enough or you don't have the voice for what God's calling you to do. When Moses argued with God in Exodus 3 and 4 that he had issues and shouldn't be the one to go to Pharaoh to save the Hebrews, God promised him that He would be his voice. If you just let God speak through you, it will be His words and His breath making the sound to get the people ready for their Savior.

Position yourself for prayer and allow your heart to connect with Jesus!

Lord, Your blood has a voice, and it speaks over me, my family, and my life! Jesus, show me the areas of my heart that keep me from the revelation of who You are. Help me to be a lover of truth, not distracted by any other sounds or people or by a false perception of who You have created me to be. I repent for believing the lie that I am a nobody, or that Your blood is not enough for me. Forgive me for partnering with the enemy in any area that would keep me bound to my flesh. I uproot all seeds of doubt that I have allowed to be planted in me that say I am not qualified to release Heaven on earth! I know that Your blood covers a multitude of sin. I know I am Your child and Heaven is my home. Let me understand and be in awe of You and all of Heaven. Jesus, I ask and invite You to correct me, to check my spirit when I grieve You. Don't allow me to walk in error. I want to be whole in Your truth, Jesus! Breathe on me, so that I may carry Your breath and Your sound in the earth and so that I may manifest as Your child here and now. Set me up, Jesus, and teach me to make You famous everywhere I go! Amen!

CHAPTER 10

Molecules of
HEAVEN

Sometime in the early hours of January 20, 2017, a wind came into my bedroom and I heard a sound coming from the wind. I asked out loud, "Holy Spirit, is this the sound You have been teaching me about?" Immediately, I was standing in the garden again. I was near the trees I had seen before, but Caleb and I walked past them and down along the riverbank.

We arrived into a field where there were all kinds of fruits and vegetables. Caleb picked up what looked like a ruby but it was actually a fruit about the size of a large apple. It appeared to be almost transparent due to its purity. He said, "The most valuable things on earth have that value because of the substance they are made of," and then he compared the substances of several things I could relate to like gold and diamonds.

Next, he began to describe how human beings are comprised of the substance of God. He picked up another fruit that I thought was a large pear. This one looked like an emerald, and he handed it to me and said, "You have to understand that the substance of Heaven resides on the inside of you. He is your substance so you (all Christians) are carriers of Heaven. He wants you to know that one of the ways He will release Heaven on earth is by it being birthed out of His people. It flows from the innermost parts of who you are, from the river in your belly." (I knew Caleb was talking about the river in John 7:38.)

He spoke in depth about the substance, the composition of all things on earth, and how that substance actually originated in Heaven because God spoke all things into existence. He explained that the power of Heaven is knowing what we are made of. Then he said, "He formed you in your mothers' wombs, but you were 'pre-formed' in Heaven. He is the Creator, and everyone is formed in His image and likeness, even if they never know Him or receive Him. When they receive Jesus, Holy Spirit forms the river in them and then when Holy Spirit baptizes them, that river inside them is activated to flow out of them."

Caleb continued, "Through the laying on of your hands on other people, you cause the heavenly substance in you to bond with the substance in them." In the way he described this, it seemed like he meant on a molecular or cellular level. Then he said, "When two come together and agree about anything they ask, it will be done for them by the Father in Heaven. A touch from Him changes the very thing or issue into the perfection of what the Creator meant it to be from the time of its very beginning."

While still staring at the beauty and purity of His creation, the truth of what I was being taught about the power of His touch fell on me like a heavy weight, and I had such a new revelation of the importance of agreement. The loving touch of Jesus brings healing, deliverance, peace, and everything else you could ever need. I could see in my spirit the look of pure desperation of the woman with the issue of blood, longing to reach her Healer, and just the touch of His very garment brought new life and vitality to her. I got lost thinking of all the times God had used people in my life to hug me, to pat me or hold my hand, or even to lay hands on me for prayer, and how those simple acts of contact were a touch from Jesus Himself, by the power of the Holy Spirit through that particular person. I remembered how, in many of those occasions, it had brought deliverance to me or whatever it was in that moment when only Jesus knew what I needed most.

Caleb took my hand and led me further along the riverbank to a place where the water shifted into a downward flow, leading in the direction of the earth. It was pooling up around the edge of the atmosphere of Heaven, and then you could see a small stream from that pool falling into the atmosphere of earth. As we watched the water trickle down onto different areas of the earth, I noticed that when a drop hit the ground, the area around the point of contact would vibrate from that touch from Heaven, as if it was a dry and thirsty land suddenly soaking in new life.

Even though it only appeared as a trickle to my eyes, the sound of the water gathering in Heaven and flowing down toward earth was like a raging waterfall and as it entered the planet's atmosphere, it was shifting the spiritual climate of that area. One drop could literally cover what looked like a whole continent, while other drops would specifically cover just one city or even a single home. The water was crystal clear, but as it left Heaven's atmosphere it carried colors that I have never seen before. It also had a heavier consistency than normal water, and it carried weight as it fell onto earth with force. There was nothing that could have stopped this flow from Heaven.

As I stood there in such awe of the flow itself, a host of angels came from above where Caleb and I were standing and they were descending down to the earth along with the flow of water. They appeared to be bringing a message, some with worshiping sounds roaring out of them and some with weapons on their bodies. Behind them was a ray of light that was penetrating through everything it came across. This light made everything it passed through become transparent. It was as if this light had an assignment from the throne room of cleansing, reformation, order, and holiness.

As the light passed over me it shone on areas in my heart that I knew were not supposed to be there, areas that I had forgotten about. It exposed places where I had taken in a lie and allowed it to plant in my thought process and even in my soul. Holy Spirit whispered to me and said, "If you allow Him to have those areas, they will no longer hold a place in your heart." I began to feel the pull of the Holy Spirit and His breeze against my heart, so very gentle, but with great desire for all that was unclean or impure in me to be blown away! Kneeling in the presence of Holy Spirit and the convicting light of Jesus, I surrendered those things one by one. The Spirit would talk to me about each place and then I would feel the flow of the river rush into those empty spots and then His love began to talk to my heart! His love has a voice and it carries more weight than anything else we might believe about ourselves or whatever lie we might have received about us, when we surrender those things and give space for His love to speak.

Caleb began to collect my tears as Holy Spirit ministered to me. He spoke life into my heart, reviving areas that I did not even know were dead. Holy Spirit breathed life into me from head to toe. "Live in Him again. Sing for Him again," I heard Him whisper over me.

Then Caleb said, "This is what is being released on the earth. There is a flood of Him coming, but first you must live again, sing again, come back to your first love again. His voice of love is calling out to you and His bride. Does the bride hear her groom? Does the creation know its Creator's voice? His way is easy. His yoke is weightless. Turn to Him in this hour and let Him correct you, allow Him to build His house again, allow Him to speak again, allow Him to lead again."

Then a voice came from Heaven like the roar of thunder, "Who do you say that I am?" The earth shook as His voice penetrated the atmosphere. It vibrated the ground and carried the power to rearrange mountains. Still kneeling, I heard Him again ask, "Who do you say that I am?"

I cried out with a loud voice, "You are the Christ, the Son of God, the one true God, my personal friend!" It came up out of me before a thought could cross my mind. My spirit was alive and free to speak.

Holy Spirit said, "This is the question lingering over the body of Christ. Who do you say that I am?" The next moment I was back in my room.

I was in awe and silence, still feeling the effects of the light I saw and the sounds of the flowing river and breath of God blowing on and around me. I know that, more than ever before, we are in the hour of needing to know for sure the answer to the question, "Who is God to you?" Who is your God? Do you believe in Him? Do you know who you are in Him? Do you know that He created you in the palm of His hand? That He formed you in His very image? Not in the sense that our natural mind could comprehend, but in our DNA, our structure, our makeup, every molecule of our bodies. The very fiber of Him is in us and is who we are in Him. He is looking for His sons and daughters to come into His reformation, to increase in the knowledge of good—His good.

As I further processed this download I received, I was looking out my window watching the wind blow and the rain pour down outside, and I smiled up toward Heaven knowing the rain of God is being released over us. Do you really know Him? Can you sense when He is near you? Is your very being aware of when its Creator walks into the room with you? And when He does, what is your response? Who do you say He is in your life? Who is He in your home? At your job? In your worship? Can others hear Him and see Him in you?

The Bible says in Joshua 24:15 to "choose for yourselves this day whom you will serve." Are you choosing Him? You have choices every day whether to partner with the enemy's plan for you or God's plan, but God's plan is *so* much better! When those choices come up, just stop for a moment and allow Holy Spirit to direct you to the right decision because His way is right every time.

A huge part of defeating the enemy in your life is the knowledge and understanding of who Jesus is to you and who you are to Him. From the beginning, God has created you to be with Him. He created you for relationship. As I've said several times, Satan has no ability to create anything, so he wants to steal everything God has made, including you! We must understand that every molecule in us, every cell, was made for a specific purpose, and that we as people also have very specific assignments. We were created to represent Him on the earth.

He has assigned the angel armies to be at your beck and call at any time. Jesus said in Matthew 26:53 that He could ask for "legions of angels," and we have the same access to those angels as well. Satan does not want you to be aware of the authority you have over the spirit realm and the power you have with the name of Jesus and the blood of the cross. He wants to weaken your voice, to steal your fight so that you roll over and die, but we have the ability to push back darkness and evil plots against us and others. If you will partner with Heaven and the book God wrote about you, and you allow Holy Spirit to have free reign in your life, you can truly be a whole person. When I say whole, I mean completely free to be who God called you to be. You can live with a heart healed and a spirit alive and well, fulfilling all that God has for you.

A true understanding of what you're made of will change your life. We are made to be carriers of God's glory! He placed and numbered every hair on your head (see Matt. 10:30). He placed Heaven on the inside of you, not just in the spirit man but in your very substance at the cellular level. Your heart and other organs and every tissue of your body were made by Him to be like Him! So when you are in need of healing, the One who created you came and took stripes on His back so that His blood would restore you to wholeness and the perfect health He created you to have and to live in.

While I was standing there in Heaven, I remember feeling the importance of what I was learning, and something so very profound happened. I received a new understanding that His truth comes with weight. The Spirit of Truth comes with the backing of Heaven. So why is it that sometimes when we hear the truth, we don't listen or don't respond?

I asked Holy Spirit, "Why is this happening? Why is there no evidence of Your presence on things that should carry glory on them?"

His response to me was, "The vessel determines the measure of weight it can hold." Satan wants to cheapen certain words here on earth, words that were created in Heaven. Many have lost their ability to access the glory of God because of their misuse and abuse of the gift or gifts God has given them. Connecting a gift without character and words without purity to the Spirit of Truth equals no power and therefore no weight.

Here is an example. In Acts 16:16-17, a slave girl was following Paul and Silas around the city as they preached and she said, "These men are the servants of the Most High God, who proclaim to us the way of salvation." This was a true statement, but it was coming from someone who had an evil spirit so it had no weight of Heaven or glory on it. In fact, it irritated Paul so much he eventually cast the spirit out of the girl.

The opposite example was Moses. God sent him with a word to tell Pharaoh to release the Hebrews and he was empowered by God Himself to deliver it. Because Heaven was behind him, Moses brought with him awesome signs and wonders—the power of God was in full display. Lord, make us vessels that can hold the weight of the oil!

I am still walking this out in my own life, inviting the Spirit of Truth to always make Heaven's plan and purpose known to me in all areas so that everything I do has that power behind it. Even Jesus said, "I speak to you timeless truth. The Son is not able to do anything from himself or through my own initiative. I only do the works that I see the Father doing, for the Son does the same works as his Father" (John 5:19 TPT). Jesus was directly connected to Heaven, and as He walked around from place to place His gaze was on the Father so He always knew what to do and when to do it. Our prayer should be, "Father let me see You so I can do what I see You do. Let my thoughts be Your thoughts and my ways Your ways."

This taught me we can come into agreement with Jesus over our lives and that agreement then gives us a level of authority of Heaven here on the earth. We have to be in unity with what the Spirit of God is saying and then speak the same thing over the earth, our cities, our churches, our families, and our own selves. We must see what the Father sees for us and hear what He is speaking to us.

As I watched the river of Heaven gathering into a pool, I could only imagine what that might look like when it is fully released on earth. What is only a trickle in Heaven is a rushing waterfall on the earth that makes Niagara Falls look like a drop in the bucket. One thing Holy Spirit asked me while I was praying about this encounter was, "Where will you be when this outpouring lands on the earth?" That question stayed on my heart for days, and you should ask yourself the same thing because it is coming soon. Where will you be? I want to be ready. I want to be directly under that water as it pours out. There will be those who are so cold toward the things of Heaven that they would miss a shift of the atmosphere over their region. Don't get complacent and don't allow your hearts to harden. Make sure there are no dusty Jesus statues on your shelves and ask the Lord not to let you miss His breath and His Spirit being poured out.

This will be like nothing we have ever seen or experienced before, nothing that can be explained in the natural. The Word of God says that His Spirit will be poured out on all flesh. No one will be able to say that His Spirit has not touched them; it will happen in a way that is undeniable. I believe that all of Heaven is watching as the water is gathering. When this outpouring comes on the earth, regions, cities, churches, and individual lives will be impacted in a way that can only be described as holy, as pure Jesus. His love impacts us so deeply, in a place only our Father can touch. His outpouring will shake our very being! It will vibrate the ground we walk on like a holy earthquake that will return people to the revelation that He is Lord, the Creator of all things, and He is the one who gave us life.

In that moment, the pure light of who He is will shine on the innermost parts of our hearts. The light can show us where we have hidden things from ourselves and Him, things that need to be exposed or washed away by His cleansing blood. His glory is in His light, and as it shines on us we will have a choice to walk with Him hand and hand as we release anything that is not of Him. Anything that the enemy has planted in you must be removed and given over to Jesus and He will receive you as His bride. As the angel said to me, you must return to your first love. Just lock your gaze on the One with the eyes of fire.

He is calling us to come and encounter Him. He longs for you. He sent His Son to die for you, He sent His Holy Spirit to walk with you, and now He is ready to bring you to Himself. Just listen to His voice and ignore all others. Speak His name and all of Heaven will come to attention.

After this we can truly answer that question God is asking us all, "Who do you say I am?" How can we answer this question without even knowing Him? Who is He to you? What has He done for you? Until you really meet Him, you have nothing to say to those questions. Your answer without that encounter with Him is, "He is a stranger. I do not know Him or anything about Him," but seek Him and you will find Him. Your soul longs for Him so just invite Him in. He will sweep over you and take you to a place of wholeness that only comes by His amazing grace and the blood of Jesus. When you walk with Him, you will always be able to resist the devil in your life. Partnering with the Kingdom of God changes your lifestyle. Partnering with Him allows you to live in the place where everything happens "on earth as it is in Heaven." Only then can we walk in the place of His love pouring out of us so that all men will be drawn unto Him in whom they may be saved.

Today, like never before, we must be able to emphatically answer that question when we hear the Father ask it. Who is He? He is our Lord. He is our Savior. He is our source, our everything. Let Him walk with you in the cool of the day. Let Him be everything to you, too.

CHAPTER 11

Chain of
COMMAND

B efore we move to the final chapter of this book, there are a few other things to cover.

There are many ways to obtain information and increase knowledge. Obvious examples are reading, going to a trade school, or maybe attending a university. Once you find something you really like, you might even pursue a Master's degree or PhD.

Another way to learn is through experience, actually practicing or doing something while you are learning it. Sometimes that might be through an apprenticeship, watching and helping someone who has already mastered the subject, until you become competent enough to do it yourself. I am personally one of those people who learns much better by experience, getting my hands dirty and figuring out how to do whatever I want or need to learn.

The best way to learn for a believer, however, is to simply listen to Holy Spirit and be a student of the Word of God. At the last supper, Jesus says to the disciples:

But the Helper (Comforter, Advocate, Intercessor—Counselor, Strengthener, Standby), the Holy Spirit, whom the Father will send in My name [in My place, to represent Me and act on My behalf], He will teach you all things. And He will help you remember everything that I have told you (John 14:26 AMP).

Notice that He says "all things." Not some things. Not a few things. All things, from the simplest to the most complex.

When I invite Holy Spirit to begin teaching me about a particular topic, He always uses examples or pictures because He knows that is the way I learn best. It is a process that usually takes time and patience. For example, as I was first beginning to understand and flow in the prophetic realm, He had to show me clearly when it was His voice that I was hearing.

I used to work for a car dealership doing title work. One of my tasks was to go to the DMV (where I lived at the time they were called tax collector's offices) to turn in titles and to pick up license plates for people who had purchased a new car. A person walks in the door, takes a number, and waits for one of the clerks to call them up. It was normally crowded so I usually had to sit in the waiting room for quite a while every time I went. One day I had just taken my number and grabbed a chair when a young lady walked in and, instantly, I knew she had walked there and that she had recently had a baby. I laughed inside at the thought and told myself I was being silly.

It wasn't long before my number was called and shortly after that the young lady was also called up to the clerk right next to me. I was trying to mind my own business and not eavesdrop, but, after the clerk had reviewed her paperwork, she told the young lady she was missing some of the documents required to get her plates and her car could not be driven until the plates were issued. The young lady started to cry and said, "Ma'am, please! I walked here and I just had a baby. I need my car!"

I literally almost fell out of my chair, and I immediately heard Holy Spirit say to me, "See, that is Me speaking to you."

Things like that started happening everywhere I went. I would be in a grocery store checkout line beside someone and instantly know something about them, and then a few minutes later hear them say the thing I knew. This went on for years and Holy Spirit showed me that I was in a training time to trust His voice. Since then, I have gone through other "trainings" like that for other topics. The key is to ask and invite the Spirit of Truth into all things, all areas of our lives. Become a lover of truth and this will set you up for great success.

When you have a true and clear knowledge about something, it is not so overwhelming or scary. I would not want to have a tire blow out when I am driving by myself because I have no idea how to change a tire, but if my husband was with me something like that would be no big deal because he is very handy and knows exactly what to do. Knowledge can bring you peace in an otherwise frustrating or aggravating situation. In the very next verse after He promised the coming of Holy Spirit, Jesus said:

> *Peace I leave with you; My [own] peace I now give and bequeath to you. Not as the world gives do I give to you. Do not let your hearts be troubled, neither let them be afraid. [Stop allowing yourselves to be agitated and disturbed; and do not permit yourselves to be fearful and intimidated and cowardly and unsettled]* (John 14:27 AMPC).

His peace. I have thought about this scripture many times and thought about all the things He could have said in that very important moment. He said, "I leave you My peace." He is the ultimate knower of all things and He has a peace that we could never understand. He sent us the greatest teacher and He left us His peace. I believe that the two walk together—that His truth brings knowledge and having knowledge is how we can walk in that type of peace. Jesus knew the enemy would attack him in many different ways while He was on earth, but He was in total peace because He knew and understood His authority. He knew who would win at the end and He would come back with the keys to the gates of hell. He has told us the end also, so if we really believe what the Bible says, we know that Satan and all his demonic forces will end up in the lake of fire for all of eternity. What a peace from knowing that! And we can rest in the same peace from every promise in His Word.

This is why we absolutely must increase our spiritual IQ and gain as much knowledge about Satan's plans and strategies as possible. I believe one of the key areas we must understand about the battle against the enemy is the ranking or order in the spirit realm. Most Jewish scholars agree that Paul gives us a picture of demonic ranks in Ephesians 6:12, which says, "For we do not wrestle against flesh and blood, but against principalities, against powers, against the rulers of the darkness of this age, against spiritual hosts of wickedness in the heavenly places." Let's start at the bottom and work our way up through the ranks, and, as you read this part, keep in mind that the Jesus inside you is so much greater than the enemy that's in this world!

When you were conceived God assigned an angel to you, to guard you and help you throughout your life, but I believe you were also assigned a demonic spirit by the enemy, to steal your calling and to keep tabs on you, to constantly buffet and irritate you. The enemy has studied people for thousands of years, so he knows exactly how to annoy and frustrate you. While demons have no access to read your mind or thoughts, they are experts on body language and they listen to every word that comes out of your mouth.

So this spirit that is assigned to you at birth is a low-level principality—not very big and not very powerful at first, and only grows in size and strength if you give it permission. One day Holy Spirit showed me this clearly. I was standing in front of my bathroom mirror and started to have some odd and troubling symptoms in my body. Suddenly there was a huge demon standing behind me, with a massive oblong-shaped head and broad shoulders. He had beady eyes and appeared quite muscular. He was much taller than me and bowed up, ready to attack. I would really relate his overall appearance to a cartoon character of some sort, but he was intimidating at first. My initial response was a righteous anger and I said, "Who do you think you are, coming up in my house without permission?"

I immediately took authority over the devil by the name of Jesus and told the devil to leave. As I rebuked him, he started shrinking, like the air was being let out of him like a balloon. Finally, he was reduced to the size of a gnat, and just buzzing around my head, and Holy Spirit said to me, "That is his true size. You can just flick him away," so I literally flicked him with my finger and he was instantly gone.

That little "gnat" spirit then reports to a local territorial spirit. This spirit may be in charge of a single street or neighborhood. If you start to increase your prayer life or do anything to increase your spiritual authority, that local spirit is alerted and you will notice a temporary difficulty in pressing in and focusing during prayer. Once you overcome that and go a little bit deeper with God, that local spirit runs and tells a regional spirit, or as Paul calls them, "powers." They are stronger and cover more area than the principalities.

A lower regional spirit is usually over a city or maybe a county. For example, hovering in the Atlanta, Georgia area, there are regional spirits of addiction and religion. These types of spirits were granted access to their specific areas long before any of us were around. Higher level regional spirits can be over an entire state or even larger area, and those spirits report to a team of special demons that control whole geographical areas and even entire nations. Those demonic teams are the "rulers of the darkness," and they are very powerful because of the authority granted to them by Satan himself. It can take a significant amount of time of prayer and intercession from a large group of unified believers to push back these types of forces in a country, but in America they have been gaining ground on us because of our division and complacency.

Finally, the strongest demonic forces on the earth are the "spiritual hosts of wickedness in heavenly places." Ephesians 2:2 refers to the enemy as the "prince of the power of the air" or "the dark ruler of the earthly realm who fills the atmosphere with his authority" (TPT). Satan and his generals occupy this space, scheming and plotting and causing destruction across the entire world. We also know he has this power because, in order to offer the "kingdoms of the world" to Jesus in Matthew 4:8-9, he had to actually be able to give them up from his own control. These spiritual hosts are serious demons and must not be taken lightly.

Quick review of the ranks:

- "Gnat" spirit or low-level, local principality— assigned to you at birth

- Territorial spirit, higher-level principality— specific to a local area

- Regional spirits, powers—usually over an area about the size of a city or county

- Regional "team" spirits, rulers of darkness—over larger areas, regions, or entire nations

- Spiritual hosts of wickedness—able to function across the entire world

There are things you can do to get reported up the enemy's chain of command quickly. It could be something as simple as asking Holy Spirit to teach you more about the spiritual realm, an increase in praying in the Spirit, or even just reading this book. How much they notice you depends directly on your spiritual temperature, and that is why the Lord said to John in Revelation 3:15-16 that He would rather we be hot or cold than lukewarm.

Because of His love for us, Jesus wants to protect us from the enemy's attacks. He knows that if we are cold, we are no threat to the devil's kingdom and Satan will leave us alone. If we are hot, we are a major threat, but we have the knowledge and understanding of our authority through Jesus Christ to stand against the attacks. If we are just lukewarm, however, that is when we are inviting more demonic activity into our lives because he wants to try to keep us from ever getting truly hot for the Kingdom of God.

As a parent, I would never want one of my children to fight against an enemy that they couldn't defeat. This is the Father's heart toward us as well and He knows exactly how the enemy works, so He doesn't want us fighting without the proper weapons or knowledge of how to win. He would actually rather us be totally cold than to expose ourselves as prey.

Of course, what God really wants is for us to burn for Him, to be totally on fire, but He wants us to have the knowledge of our power to overcome Satan before we even show up on the enemy's radar. Don't let the devil lie to you about this. You can walk in the same authority as Jesus Himself over your family, your business, your ministry, and every area of your life, but you have to know how to use that authority. If I had a million dollars in the bank, but didn't know how to access the money or even the bank account, I still wouldn't be able to pay my bills and I would suffer for it. But, once I figured out how to write a check or use my debit card, I would have no problem paying those bills.

It is the same thought process with spiritual things. We all have the same authority, but some of us learn how to use it and some of us are too lazy to learn. Again, He does not want us to be ignorant of spiritual things. He wants us to go to the school of the Word of God. He wants us to take time to learn of Him and His Kingdom. Why do you think He said to ask Him for His Kingdom to come, His will to be done on earth as it is in Heaven? He said that so we would take spiritual things seriously because that knowledge is life or death for us as believers.

Knowing Him will show you who you are in Him. Again, remember how Jesus talks in John 17 about us being "in Him" just like He was in the Father and the Father was in Him. Getting a hold of this will give you such an increased hunger for more *of* Him and to be more hidden *in* Him. When you submit your flesh and who you are to who He is, the more "in Him" you become, and this is how you actually find your true self, the one who was formed in your mother's womb. He knows us in a way we can't understand. We carry who He is in us, so to know Him is to start to understand who and what He made you to be. I believe this is the truest picture of dying to self, or as the Word says in Matthew 10:39, you have to lose your life so you can find it.

The enemy wants to set us up so we find the wrong path, and we lose our life to pain and suffering, disappointments, and so on. One of the keys to staying on the right path with Jesus is to not allow the things of this world to stay on us. Be quick to leave your pains and aggravations at His feet. Be quick to repent for bitterness or unforgiveness. The longer we allow these types of things to rule our hearts or minds, the further the door opens for the enemy and his minions to come in and torment you.

I am sure you're thinking to yourself, "That's easier said than done," or "You don't know what I have been through in my life." You're right, I don't know what you have been through and I am sure if we had the chance to sit together and share, we would swap stories and both be shocked over the different things we have survived. You have to stop looking at what seemed to cause you pain and/or hurt because that's just the enemy keeping your focus off of the Healer and Deliverer. See, if he can keep your eyes on yourself or the things of the world then you will stay bound and keep going around the same mountain over and over again, but Jesus never said to go around the mountain; He said to tell the mountain to move!

The Lord spoke to me and said, "Your focus cannot be split between Me and your pain during Your time of healing." See, I was trying to get to a place of freedom on my own without allowing Holy Spirit to really do the work in me that needed to be done. What was really happening was I wanted to hold on to the pain because it gave me permission to mistreat others around me. I thought it gave me a reason to keep walls up with everyone, and I could protect myself from the bad people that way. But that is not freedom at all; you are actually telling God, "I don't trust You to protect me or defend me." Maybe you blame God for allowing something to happen to you, which is a very dangerous place to be. God wants to heal all of your broken places, to the deepest parts of who you are. You must put all your hope and faith in Him and stop meditating on the pain if you want true freedom. At the end of this chapter I have included a prayer to allow Holy Spirit to start revealing past things that maybe you have forgotten about so you can release them and allow Him to heal those wounds inside of you.

Earlier in the book I said that the enemy can try to place a haze over our eyes and then bring confusion to break our focus on God. You also see how the enemy came after the young girl with a plan to administer what he calls the death blow, but that death blow is only able to come into our lives after the enemy has successfully stolen our will. Remember, the death blow is not always to take you out physically but, even more important to the enemy, to get you to throw your hands in the air and give up completely. Give up on your dreams and your passions. His goal is to take away your ability to be effective for the Kingdom of God and to make you as miserable as possible in the meantime. The enemy loves to mock God in any area possible, so if he can get you to be sick or unhappy while we are here in his kingdom, he will do that as much as we allow him.

The enemy sets the same plan in motion for all of us—to steal, kill, and destroy, in that order. Holy Spirit said to me one time, "Who can steal something from you that you don't have?" and in my mind I saw a thief come to a house that was vacant and he just turned around and left because there was nothing inside to take. So, I understood more clearly that when the enemy comes it is because I have something that he wants me *not* to have. Just as the Bible says the enemy comes to steal the seed of the Word, when we are saved there are spirits released immediately to come steal that salvation from you. Why? Because as we receive Christ into our hearts, there are also deposits put inside of us of faith, joy, peace, love, a prophetic voice, and so much more. When the Lord moves inside of you, He brings all His stuff, so now the thief has something to steal.

The first thing the enemy comes for is your joy, because the joy of the Lord is your strength. Satan only works in our weakness because when we are strong he is scared that we might use our authority over him. After he takes your joy and your strength, he goes after your peace. He can lie to you to quickly take your peace of mind and make you confused, worried, and doubtful your salvation is even real.

Next, the enemy goes after your ability to receive love or give love. He does this many ways but the most common is through hurt. Satan does his best to get you around the wrong people to bring what everyone calls "church hurt" so you run away from the family of God. If he makes it this far, he can get us to tune out the voice of God and follow the voices of the people around us that he has placed there to influence us and then he has you right where he wants you. You're weak, broken, depressed, probably lonely, and desperate, and then he moves to phase two of the attack.

The demons call the second phase the "kill zone," meaning they kill your dreams, your hopes, and your desire to fight or stand for anything. All of this is to get to your will. See, your will is where you still have the ability to pull yourself up by the boot straps and get yourself together and make a turn back to the Lord, so they want you to give up on your will to follow the call of God on your life, or your will to even live at all. The enemy wants to kill your destiny and move you into the final phase of his attack.

Phase three is to literally destroy you, to deliver that "death blow." This can come when you're 10, 30, or 80; the enemy is no respecter of age. I have seen many that seem so close to ending well when a death blow takes them out early. And remember, although it sometimes is, it doesn't have to be a physical death.

Have you ever seen a powerful ministry suddenly fall apart? They may be doing all kinds of things for the Lord or at least in His name, but in the background that pastor or ministry leader is actually struggling or even in sin. They are in phase two and the enemy is on their tail to take them out so they stop being effective for the Kingdom of God. The death blow is shortly behind if they don't make the right choices to change.

The great news, the amazing news, is that you never have to experience that death blow. When you understand your authority and the power of the Kingdom you have access to, then the enemy can never get to you to steal anything from you. It's like having a security system on your home or car. If someone starts to break in a window or open a door without a key, then all the alarms start going off, alerting you and everyone around you that someone is trying to steal from you.

This is why the enemy tries quickly to separate you from the body of Christ and other believers—if you're around others who understand the sounds of the alarms, then they begin to run to your rescue and to alert you if you don't hear it yourself. If you're reading this now and you're not spending time with the family of God because someone offended you, then that's an alarm that you're in phase two of the attack. The enemy is in your camp. Kick him out and get yourself back to church and find a group of people you can call family.

I hope you can see now how the enemy has come up against you and how you have not fought back correctly. Remember, he can't come up with anything new, so he just keeps repeating his same old patterns. Learn to recognize the signs of an attack. When you see them, don't just go with the flow because that is a dangerous place or position to be in. That means you are just allowing the devil to take you for a ride, like getting in the car with no steering wheel to drive it. Why would anyone in their right mind do that?

The enemy wants control of your mind so that you fall prey to his plan to take you down a road you never meant to go on. My sweet momma would always say, "Sin will take you farther than you want to go," and that is such a true statement. I saw this in my own life many times and I would look up from what I was doing or what was around me and think to myself, "How did I get here?" or "This is not who I am." In those moments I knew I was not in control of my life, but I had moved into the back seat and allowed someone else to take over.

There are many signs, or "red flags" as I like to call them, that the enemy is actively working in your life. Here are some of the symptoms:

- Constantly feeling tired, no matter how much you have rested

- Being easily annoyed, no matter how simple or unimportant the reason

- Unable to stay focused

- Lack of vision or purpose

- No laughter in your life

- Dreading tomorrow

- Never feeling accomplished

- Feeling overwhelmed with even small issues or life in general

- No real desire to pray or worship or read your Bible

- No excitement about anything

- Always feeling like you're never getting ahead financially

- Godly people around you irritate you or get on your nerves for no reason

- Resentment of others' joy or peace

- No motivation for things that you used to enjoy

- No passion for anything or anyone

- Feeling sick in your body

- Feeling like you're in a daze

- Losing track of time

- Feeling like you need worldly things to "unwind" or relax (i.e. drinking alcohol, watching hours of meaningless TV, spending hours on social media, etc.)

- Feeling happier to be alone than around others

If you recognized any of those signs, then you could be on the road to complete burnout or the death blow.

Let's look at one of them specifically so we can expound on how this works. One of the most common attacks from the enemy is to make you feel sick in your body. This can be anything from a toothache to a terminal disease, but remember that the enemy only has permission to bring sickness in your body if you have given it to him. You might say, "I *never* gave him permission!" and it's not like you stood at your door and said, "Come on in devil!" But he doesn't usually walk in your front door; he is a thief so he checks for back doors, windows, or even the tiniest cracks to come through.

Sickness always begins with some type of symptom, maybe a slight pain or a runny nose or it could be something more intense. I think of it like this—if someone is knocking on my door, do I let them in or tell them to go away, or do I just ignore them, hoping they go away on their own? When the enemy tries to put a symptom on you, there is a word you need to say to him and that word is "*No!*" When that knock comes on your door, you leave the door bolted shut and say, "No devil!" Tell him he has no place touching your body, your mind, or your emotions. The Bible says in James 4:7 to "Resist the devil and he will flee from you." Well, not answering the door is resisting him. Rebuke the spirit of pain and command it to leave you and your household alone in Jesus's name! That spirit has no choice but to go from me. Remember, everything that has a name has to bow to the name of Jesus. Cancer has a name, diabetes has a name, any symptom that has a name can be cast out! Then thank the Lord that you are healthy and whole and ask Holy Spirit to comfort and strengthen you.

Like I said, even if you don't answer the door, the enemy looks for other ways to get in. Here are a few potential openings for the enemy to work in our lives:

- Unforgiveness

- Bitterness

- Anger

- Hate

- Disappointment

- Frustration

- Hurt

- Sin

- Partnering with wrong spirits

- Open practice of anything demonic

- Constantly putting other things before your time with the Lord

All of these are portals or pathways open to the enemy to come in and torment us with any of the symptoms or issues that I listed before. One time I was in the middle of a move from one state to another state. The movers had arrived and were almost finished taking the last pieces out of the home. Two of the movers had not been very careful with our furniture and in fact had hit a wall earlier in the day, damaging both the wall and my dresser. As the day progressed I was getting more and more annoyed. I actually said to the Lord, "I am so frustrated," and I felt His conviction immediately. I went quickly into the bathroom and asked Him why I felt that, and He spoke to me and said, "Get rid of it." I was slightly confused, so He began to remind me that anything that has a name that is not of Him has to bow and go from us, but if we allow it to remain and fester the enemy has a string attached to it and he can get in through that opening, even later on. I began to release all the aggravation and frustration, asking the Lord to help me live my life in all situations with the fruits of the Spirit as Galatians 5 talks about. Suddenly I felt His peace return and I left the bathroom with joy in my heart and excitement flooded my thoughts.

Now you might think, "This is stupid" and that I had every right to be annoyed and so forth, but you see we are not of this world so why would I allow myself to get worked up over something so petty? How many times have you caught yourself at the point of anger for really no reason? Have you seen your overreaction about some situation or even lashing out toward someone cause them to experience hurt from you? I can think of so many examples where I have fallen into this trap of the enemy, to take something so tiny and turn it into a huge issue in my life. God wants us to live by the fruit of the Spirit, in the ways of His Kingdom, not of the enemy's kingdom. When we learn of His ways and start living as sons and daughters of His Kingdom, we will never want to go back to any other way or lifestyle. You will never have to worry about any open areas in your life for the enemy to come in when you step into God's world.

Look at that list again and ask Holy Spirit to open your eyes to see where you might have left doors open or allowed the enemy to come in and take you on a path you had no intention of ever being on. Speaking from my own experiences, that path could have taken you into places or relationships that you would normally in your right thinking never have gotten yourself into, but it is such an easy process to remove yourself from the current road and get back into the perfect will of God for your life.

Holy Spirit will start bringing things to your mind He wants you to let go or repent over. I can give you another example here. In my process of letting go of past hurts, the Holy Spirit reminded one day me of a teacher I had in the second grade, many years ago. She really was a hurting woman and in turn she would hurt those around her, and I became one of her victims. She had repeatedly abused me verbally and one day in class had even smacked my hand with a wooden ruler!

I had long forgotten about her and any pain and unforgiveness that I had hidden in my heart toward her, but as soon as Holy Spirit brought it up, I could feel my annoyance at even the thought of her. I said to myself, "Wow! That is not who I am anymore! Where did that come from?" I immediately repented for holding on to that and then began to pray for her and released her and that pain by praying it out of my mouth.

I should also mention this was not during my usual prayer time; I was just driving down the road on my way to work at the time. Always be listening when Holy Spirit speaks. Since then many things have come up in my memory bank that I have had to release, and I love it because the more you release, the more free you feel. It's like dropping off a heavy backpack off your back every time.

If you are in a place where you know you're fighting a symptom or some other type of spiritual attack, then take a deep breath and pray this out right now:

*Lord, somewhere in my life I have opened the door for the enemy to torment me. I ask that You come like a river and flood over me and my emotions right now and bring up anything that is not of You so I can release it and walk free with You. I repent of allowing the enemy into any area of my life. I repent of sin, for anything that I have said or done that displeased You. I repent for having fear that I have allowed to control me and influence my decisions. I stand in the authority given to me by Jesus and with the power of the Holy Spirit, and I rebuke everything that the enemy has used against me, and I say **go** from me in Jesus's name! I command all regional spirits, territorial spirits, and all other demonic forces to leave me alone and to cease all attacks against me and my family immediately. I release the ministering angels to come and minister to me right now as I walk through this process of healing. Thank You, Jesus, for who You are and teach me more about Your Kingdom and Your ways. Help me to see myself as You see me. I plead the blood of Jesus over my life, over my home, and over my family right now, and I charge the angels of the Lord to be camped around us. Holy Spirit, reveal to me clearly any open door so I can slam it shut in the devil's face and lock it for good. Thank You, Lord, for rescuing me and my family! Amen!*

Now that you have prayed that prayer, do your best to stay in the mindset of worship. Be careful what you allow in through your eye gates and ear gates. I keep worship music playing in several rooms of my home 24 hours a day, which helps to maintain the spiritual atmosphere around me. If Holy Spirit brings anything to your mind, release it quickly; you have held on too long already. It's time to be the best you—the version of yourself that's totally free. You will be more focused on what the Lord wants you to do than ever before!

CHAPTER 12

Residue of
HEAVEN

There is something that I was questioning the Lord about that is a sensitive topic for the body of Christ and is very controversial in many different groups of believers. There is significant debate about what is and is not of God, usually in Pentecostal/Charismatic circles, when Holy Spirit shows up in a service or gathering. Not to mention that people from the outside looking in sometimes think we look like crazy people or freaks who have no clue how to handle ourselves. I hate nothing more than when an unbeliever or even a baby Christian walks away from Jesus because someone runs them off by acting in a weird way.

Don't misunderstand what I am saying. I believe firmly that we will see signs and wonders, likely more and more as we get closer to Christ's return, but the primary purpose of those signs and wonders is for the unbeliever to be drawn to the Father. So if your "wonder" or the way you are acting is causing unbelievers to run away from God instead of to Him, then it is coming from your flesh and not from Heaven.

Being raised around ministry, I have seen all kinds of miracles and I truly believe God can do *anything*. I've seen blind eyes opened, deaf ears healed, people get out of wheelchairs, and, from about two feet away, a new kneecap form in a man's knee. I have also seen lots of other signs and wonders and all kinds of different reactions by people to the movement of Holy Spirit in a service. Some of it was absolutely a genuine encounter with the power of God, some of it was just emotions, and some of it was the actual manifestation of demons in reaction to God's presence. The only thing I know for certain was that Holy Spirit is a gentleman and He would never force Himself on someone or make them do something that would grieve Him.

I was taught growing up that if you cannot find something in the Word then it is not of God, but what I did not realize was that we do not always understand what we are reading in the Bible and that the Bible itself speaks in several places about the "mysteries" of the Kingdom of Heaven. We must not limit God and we cannot assume that everything we see happening around us or even to us can be completely explained by a single scripture.

Jesus did strange things that had never been seen before on earth, likely to help us understand true signs and wonders and miracles. In John 9:6, He spat on the ground, made clay out of the wet dirt, and put it on the eyes of a blind man to heal him. I don't know why He did that but maybe, as we are all made from dust, He just scooped up some brand-new eyes out of that ground! He sometimes asks us to do some out-of-the-box things as well, and if we are to do even greater things than Jesus (see John 14:12), then those greater things might still be mysteries that we cannot explain.

One of the things I was asking Holy Spirit about was the topic of what some people call gold dust. Several years ago, I had finished preaching at a service and someone came up to me saying they saw gold dust on me. I immediately dismissed it and said to the person, "Oh, no I wear perfume that has glitter in it so that's what you're seeing," which was true that particular evening. But, soon after that, I began to hear others discussing this happening in some meetings along with other things that no one could really explain. Again, I did my homework and couldn't find anywhere in the Bible where it mentioned gold dust or angel dust. I also do not believe angels are "dusty," so for years I never gave it a second thought and just stayed out of those conversations.

Then, in 2016, I heard about a service where someone I really respect in the body of Christ had something that appeared to be gold all over him and around a pulpit he was preaching from. I was not present for this event, but as he discussed it I felt the Holy Spirit on it and so I began to ask the Lord, "Help me to be open to everything You have for us here on the earth, and do not allow my little thinking to limit You on what You can do or how You manifest."

I continued praying about that for the next 30 days or so and I just kept asking Holy Spirit to teach me and to correct me. I repented and asked the Lord to forgive me if I had dismissed or even made fun of something that was actually of Him.

We have to be careful that we do not just disregard things we do not understand before seeking the Holy Spirit on all matters. We must invite the Spirit of Truth to come and teach us on every topic. Everything we need to know is found in Jesus and by giving Him full access in all areas. He will never lead us wrong. One of the biggest mistakes I have made in my lifetime is ignoring that small check in my spirit about something or someone. I would override that check and reason it out or justify my actions by telling myself, "Oh, that's just me," or, "I am sure it's fine," but Holy Spirit recently shared with me that He does not need to give me evidence on why He says yes or no to something. As my momma used to tell me all the time when I was little, sometimes the answer is just "No" and doesn't require an explanation. We either trust Him or we don't, and we get in error when we start reasoning out things that we have no business reasoning within ourselves, especially when it is a spiritual matter that Heaven is trying to release.

It was my questioning to God about all this that caused me to go on a journey with Holy Spirit and that I believe led me to this encounter.

Sometime in early February 2017, I was lost in worship, and the presence of the Lord was resting in the room and all around me. My mind was completely in submission to the Spirit of God, and I heard Holy Spirit say, "Open your eyes."

As I obeyed, I was standing with my angel, Caleb, and we were in some type of heavenly realm, looking down on an empty and very still atmosphere. It was incredibly dark, not in an evil way, but the total absence of light.

Suddenly there appeared to be a person walking toward us from quite a distance away. I could not see the details in His face and, although His general form was of a man, He was otherwise completely indescribable and I believe I was only able to see Him at all because I was not looking through an earthly lens. Even though He wasn't physically close to us, it felt as if He was surrounding us. There is absolutely no way to put it into words but I can only say His presence was perfect, and I knew I was in the presence of the Father. Tears streamed down my face as I felt His closeness and His overwhelming love. Although I wasn't allowed to see Him up close and cannot describe Him, I can tell you that there is no other love like that and no one or no thing could ever separate you from Him. I could feel every thought He had for me, and every breath He took felt like a breath within my own flesh. He knew I was there and loved my very presence. I have never felt more welcomed in my entire life in any situation and I knew that the presence of God is our truest home.

In that moment I felt sorry for all the people on the earth who were missing out on this experience and I had a flood of emotions as I was reminded that they will one day stand before their Father as well. In an instant they will know for certain He is their Father, but for many of them that realization will come too late.

In the midst of this rush of thoughts and emotions, Caleb said to me, "Watch. You have asked and now you will understand something about the gold."

I knew then that I had stepped into the scene that is described in Genesis 1:1, and I heard the Father begin to create Heaven. He simply spoke and it came into existence. He said things like, "Let there be My glory in My house," and, "Let there be many mansions in My house," and the instant He spoke the words I could see what He spoke right before my eyes. It wasn't a thought or an idea, and it wasn't a process. Every word that came from His mouth created something that was immediately tangible, in full detail, from the golden bricks in the street to each beautiful jewel in His throne.

Then I saw the "air," or the atmosphere in Heaven. When you open a window shade in your home and the sun shines into a dim room, you can see dust particles floating in the air. Similar to that, when God spoke Heaven into existence, the atmosphere there appeared to have dust floating around, but the particles were shimmering and sparkling like the purest gold. I remembered seeing this in an earlier encounter, but had not thought about it any further at that time. As I saw it this time, I said to Caleb, "It's not dust! It is the very atmosphere of Heaven!"

Holy Spirit spoke to me in that moment and said, "The atmosphere of Heaven is the aroma of the Father's glory," and I somehow understood exactly what He was saying to me.

Then Caleb turned and said, "When Heaven's atmosphere invades the earth's, the very residue of Heaven manifests in that place."

As I was looking through the air of Heaven, I caught just a glimpse of the Father's eyes as He was looking back at me. In His eyes I could see all of the beauty of Heaven and at the same time I saw all of who I am from His perspective. Every answer to every question can be found there in the reflection of the purest knowledge and wisdom. In just a quick glance from Him, you find that endless and unconditional love. I felt as though everything else stood still as I got lost in His gaze, and then I heard Holy Spirit speak to me and say, "Tell them of His love, the love in His eyes for them."

While I was still processing those words, I was taken to a different place, into what seemed like a modern lunch spot where I saw an active attack of the enemy to bring confusion to a group of young people and distract them. They all appeared to be under the age of 25 and they were there eating and fellowshipping. I could see all of the demons in the room and I also saw angels there as well. There were eight people there and almost every person had multiple angels with them. I knew from previous encounters that there are many different types of angels and I recognized that every person had a warrior angel assigned to them and most of them had what I like to call a messenger angel with them as well.

The angels were all standing still as if they were awaiting orders to be given to them, and there was one specific angel standing in the middle of the group who was assigned to that entire region. The demons in the restaurant were all different sizes and were various ranks. Each person had a demon assigned to them and, in all the cases, the demon had the same look as the person, like it was mimicking or imitating the person. If the person moved or switched positions, so would the demon. I could see that each demon was intently fixed on their assigned person. Their focus was so intense that no noise or movement around them would distract them from what they were concentrating on.

As the young people were discussing their plans for the next few days, I saw the surrounding demons scheming amongst themselves and chuckling, thinking for a moment they were succeeding with their assignment. I knew this was a group of believers and they were discussing a gathering of like-minded people, calling it a mastermind group. They had a strategy to try to capture others like them who were wanting to grow their influence within their age group in their community. I could hear their heart as they discussed this gathering with the sole purpose of leading as many as possible to encounter the genuine presence of Jesus.

The regional angel began to whisper to the other angels with the young people, and they began to release a sound over them. The sound was unique and very different from anything that I had heard before, but as the sound filled the air I could hear other angels from surrounding areas join in. My heart was filled with so much joy and you could see the joy on the faces of all the angels as well. Then it seemed as though the young people began to recognize that Heaven was filling the room, and they, too, were filled with joy and even began to laugh. The demons had no power or authority over them and their chuckling had stopped quickly as the young people had come into agreement with Heaven for their region.

Suddenly I was taken slightly higher up where I could see over the room. I could even see myself and everyone else there from above. As the sound was being released, we all began to worship. The light in the room began to increase and even the temperature shifted as Heaven began to fill the place. A physical cloud began to form in the room, and then came the aroma of Heaven that reached every corner of the building. It was as if Heaven had kissed that place, and the residue rested on each one of us. The atmosphere of Heaven I had seen earlier had been intermingled with the atmosphere in that room and there was tangible evidence it was there.

Caleb turned to me and said, "This is the Father's heart. Go into all the world, preach the Gospel, and release all of Heaven everywhere you go. They will know you are from the Father, and Heaven is your home." When he said the word *home,* I was back in my room trembling under the power of the Holy Spirit.

The stillness that was in that place before creation was like nothing I've ever experienced in the natural. I can only compare it to what I remember from science class about being in a vacuum. Only the power and presence of God can quiet your mind and body to a level that you can come closer to Him in a very intimate way. The Bible says in Psalm 46:10, "Be still, and know that I am God," and I believe to truly "know" Him we must find that place of total stillness and focus on Him completely.

I wish I could describe to you the love I felt from the Father. Although I could only see His general form and He was far away from me, it felt as if He was all around me or consuming me. I was given just a small glimpse of what being one with the Father is like and I think when I saw His eyes it was a prophetic example of the fact that, even though sometimes we think God is far away, just locking eyes with Him for a moment will pull you in close to feel His love and affection for you like never before. It was an experience I will never forget.

I am not sure why God took me to the scene from Genesis to teach me about the "gold dust," but I believe it was because He wanted to show me it is not something new but has been here since the actual beginning of time. Perhaps He knew I would comprehend it better that way and He used the analogy of letting light into a dark place because He always talks to me in a way He knows I can easily understand. I hope this will help others to understand it as well.

I still don't know if the "dust" is actually gold as we know it, but it definitely had a similar appearance. The point is that, whatever it is, it is part of Heaven itself and always has been, but the real revelation I want to get across is what Holy Spirit said to me about it being the "aroma" of the Father's glory. During the encounter, I felt like I knew what He meant, but as I was writing this down I kept thinking, "Why would He use the word *aroma*, which I think everyone associates with the sense of smell, to describe something you can touch and feel?" So, I researched the origin of the word *aroma*, which comes from the Greek for spice or fragrance, and as I dug deeper I found it was related to an ancient word, *myron,* which means a fragrant oil, and we relate oil with anointing. Holy Spirit was telling me what I was seeing was the actual remnant of the anointing and a tangible form of the fragrance of the glory of God!

Don't try to reason this out or overcomplicate it by applying a doctrine or theology to it. Quite simply, God can do anything He wants to do and if His glory truly invades a place, there will be evidence that He was there. Sometimes that evidence will be a healing miracle, sometimes it may be a marriage restored, and sometimes it could be a tangible residue that appears to look like gold or glitter. The only thing I know for certain is that when it's really His Glory, people will not leave that place the same.

Heaven is longing to come and encounter us here on earth, so that we may know the sound and feel of our true home in our innermost being. Heaven is not only the place where Jesus and the Father reside, but it is a place that is full of life and it is where we belong. It was created for the children of God and for all of His creation, and I believe we are coming to a time in history when we will see "on earth as it is in Heaven" more and more. As I saw in an earlier encounter, the "line" between Heaven and earth is thinning and barely recognizable in the spirit realm, so I believe it will become more common to see the residue of Heaven manifested in our physical world as well.

Why would it start to happen more? Why would we see an increase of the glory of God? Why would we see more signs and wonders? It's not so we can start seeking the residue itself or any other physical "sign" of His presence. It is for us to seek *Him,* and for His fame to spread as it did in the New

Testament when Jesus performed a miracle. Heaven will be manifested on the earth to draw the lost to the Father. His heart is longing for His sons and daughters to release the Spirit of Truth and all that He has placed in them to everyone on earth. He wants relationship, to enjoy the cool of the day in the garden with man again, and to fill the void in people that no other person or thing can fill. The Bible says, "But seek first the kingdom of God and His righteousness, and all these things shall be added to you" (Matt. 6:33). We must go after God and not just His glory or His gold, but if we get the order right, we may just see a lot more than we expected.

We must accept that God is vast and no one has the ability to understand all sides of Him with their natural mind. Only in the supernatural, by the Spirit of God, can we even begin to scratch the surface of who He is. You may encounter things in life, strange or unusual things that you might not understand. When you do, you must discern if it is from Jesus, or from Holy Spirit, or if it is something that is not real or is in your imagination, or if it is a false spirit trying to deceive you. You must also never try to fake something that is not genuine. As I've said before, when it comes to people, you *must* separate the person and the spirit they might have partnered with or are dealing with. This discernment could be life or death to you and you must not throw something out because you cannot understand it.

I believe the "restaurant scene" of this encounter was a reminder to me of the constant battle in the spirit realm that this book has really been about. Whether you believe it or not, there are always angels and demons around us and we must partner with the right Spirit. We cannot allow ourselves to be offended or wounded by a spirit, even if it is coming out of the mouth or from the actions of someone we love and respect. Decide today not to partner with anything that is not of Jesus. The easy test to see if it is Jesus is to ask if it is good. Is it pure and holy? Without holiness we are only encountering the Jesus we know in our mind without welcoming Him and all of who He is into our hearts and lives.

You can encounter all that your heart longs for, and it comes by invitation only, but it's a backward invitation. Instead of you having to wait to be invited to get what you want, you can actually receive all God has for you by inviting Him to come and bring it to you! All He asks is that you surrender to Him to get Him in His fullness. Check your heart and ask God what you are missing. Ask Him what He can bring to fill up any empty places in your life so there is no room for you to partner with the enemy and allow a counterfeit to come in.

As you finish this book, remember you are now responsible for the knowledge you have obtained and God will expect a lifestyle shift from you. Never stop asking Holy Spirit to come in your life; live with your heart fully open to all He wants to teach you and walk according to Galatians 5:16! Be a lover of truth and the Spirit will show you that truth in every situation. Now that you are more aware of the enemy's plans and have been reminded of how to defeat him, you must avoid any partnership with him. Don't allow the devil to bully your mind or emotions or tell you that you have to stay hidden or in a camouflaged place your whole life. He would love it if we would all stay in our homes or lost in the crowds and be ineffective for the Kingdom, so let's come out from among them and change the world.

Come with a heart of thankfulness and worship as you enter into prayer:

Create in me a clean heart, Lord; do a new thing in me that only You can do! Expose all areas of my life that are not of You—areas hidden even from myself. Breathe Your Spirit of Truth into my life and into my very being! Expose the weaknesses of my flesh so that I may repent and turn away from all those things that hurt Your heart. Don't allow me to grieve Your Holy Spirit. Help me, Lord, to partner with all that You have for my life. Help me to partner with the angels that are assigned to me to help me fulfill Your will for me and my household.

Forgive me for any false teachings that I have submitted to that are not of You! As I surrender to all of You and I lower myself before You, teach me who You are so that I may know Your heart and know Your ways. I give myself to You fully. I step out of what I understand and I remove any limits that I have ever placed on You! I disconnect with any wrong spirit. I uproot any lie that I have labeled as truth in my heart or mind. Increase in me as I surrender to Your hands! This is the season that I will be intentional toward You and make room for You and all of Heaven in my life! Heaven, come invade me now so that I might increase in the knowledge and understanding of God! Jesus, keep my eyes on Your eyes of fire and forgive me for being easily distracted away from Your gaze! I will step boldly into all that You have for me because I know that with You all things are possible and I will be able to fulfill all that You have for me. From this day forward, do not allow me to walk off the pages You have written about me in my book in Heaven. Thank You, Jesus! Amen.

Prayer of Salvation

Dear Jesus, come into my heart. Forgive me of my sins. Wash me. Change me. Set me free. Let me never be the same again. Jesus, I believe you died for me and that you rose again. Help me to live for You, and to fulfill everything you have called me to do. I thank you that because of Your blood I am now forgiven and on my way to Heaven. In Jesus name, AMEN!

If you prayed this prayer to receive Jesus, please let us know! Contact us at www.makehisnamefamous.com.

About Aprile Osborne

APRILE OSBORNE has been involved in ministry from a very young age. Her family traveled and ministered with Dr. Norvel Hayes, who is her spiritual father and mentor, along with other great men of God. By the time she was a teenager, she had been in services and crusades on four continents. As an adult Aprile worked under Brother Norvel again as his youth pastor and a teacher at his international Bible school and she began traveling to preach at various churches and conferences.

Find out more about Aprile and her ministry at
www.makehisnamefamous.com.

Made in the USA
Columbia, SC
02 June 2020